Rethinking Territorial Development Policies

A new framework for territorial stakeholders

Theory, methods and implementations

Michel Felix

SKEMA Business School, Lille University, France

and

Philippe Vaesken

IAE Lille, Lille University, France

Series in Economic Development

VERNON PRESS

www.vernonpress.com

In the Americas:	In the rest of the world:
Vernon Press	Vernon Press
1000 N West Street, Suite 1200	C/Sancti Espiritu 17,
Wilmington, Delaware, 19801	Malaga, 29006
United States	Spain

Series in Economic Development

Library of Congress Control Number: 2021932178

ISBN: 978-1-64889-297-4

Also available: 978-1-62273-525-9 [Hardback]; 978-1-64889-262-2 [PDF, E-Book]

Cover design by Vernon Press using elements designed by starline / Freepik.

Table of Contents

List of Figures

List of Tables

Introduction

Globalization is an economic and social phenomenon that tends to redefine the political spectrum of the world. The framework of ideology is now global, and the impacts of any local action is interfering with the rest of the world. It is clear that the interconnections are multiple and require a global systemic vision. Likewise, the logics and strategies of actors are no longer thought in a local context, but rather in an international one. So in local or territorial action, the issue of their relevance or consistency arises even more. Often recognized by the term "local development", this framework of actions should reconsider its modes of intervention. Resulting from the needs of territorial economic development after the Second World War, decisions aiming at territorial progress are seen as a complement of the central decisions (national or international). It allows the development of the territories badly integrated into major growth patterns and the resulting action programs. In this case, more than compensating for the weakness of the territory, it is a question of finding it a place of choice in this national and/or international spectrum for them. The development has become a real strategic axis within the framework of local policies. In this sense, it brings innovations, initiatives, and even more value creation or value co-creation.

The theme of territorial development constitutes the heart of the analysis of this book. Its purpose is to define innovative territorial development processes. The proposed approach comes from a European program (SEVENTH FRAMEWORK PROGRAM, Marie Curie Actions People: International Research Staff Exchange Scheme) called VALUES (Value Analysis of Local Utilities of Enterprises from Social Sector). This program has tested a new territorial development scheme that responds to the current problems of local development, which is presented in this work under the name "Territorial Value Framework" (TVF). So how can territorial regulation and governance optimize all forms of value creation in the context of a development process? These concepts of regulation and governance in the TVF are essential for a general understanding of the process. They lead to taking into account and closely linking a set of analyzes, such as those of stakeholders and the relational approach or that of systems for implementing public policies in an institutional framework.

The restitution, in the TVF, of the determinants of local development also calls for decision analysis, classic approaches linked to local and territorial development (Bottom-Up, Top-Down, endogenous and exogenous developments), and value co-production and co-creation in a context of combining available local resources or to-be-created ones. A methodology for analyzing and structuring a decision support system is proposed. This system integrates all these dimensions in a successive and systemic approach.

The originality of this book is to propose a global vision of the variables that explain the general dynamics of development reached by a territory and ways to strengthen and extend it. The TVF borrows from different territorial scientific approaches, such as strategic management, political analysis, marketing services to arrive at a reading, and action grids for territorial development. The connection of concepts from these disciplines is principally based on the processes of development and those of value creation.

Rethinking territorial development policies essentially implies that all stakeholders, including beneficiaries, can become actors in development through appropriate actions. Encouraging co-production, co-creation and transfer of values becomes, in the vision of the TVF, a key factor in territorial development and its sustainability. In this sense, the vision of the TVF is a specific vision. It places the mechanisms of influence and attractiveness through the value creation at the center of the assessment and conduct of development.

The approach aims to be innovative by its multidisciplinary nature. It combines the contributions of territorial management with those of territorial marketing and service marketing or those of economic sciences, such as territorial economy, regional and urban economics, political, social and geographic sciences (human geography, spatial geography ...). Of course, the proposed innovation is not a radical or breakthrough innovation, but rather an incremental innovation. It offers a new model for analyzing territories and setting up their development plan based on the construction of a new interdisciplinary reading grid: the TVF.

The presentation of this new development framework for territorial stakeholders is in stages, starting with a presentation of the key concepts and their relationships, then the methods and tools that help in the analysis and strategic choices offering a complete approach to their implementation. Three case studies are illustrated to test the relevance of the proposed approach. The book is in 7 chapters that help to understand the construction of the method and its applicability. These chapters are:

Chapter 1: Governance, regulation and territorial policies.
Chapter 2: New strategical design for territorial development.
Chapter 3: Method and Tool 1: The Territorial Value Framework (TVF).
Chapter 4: Method and Tool 2: The Stakeholders Analysis.
Chapter 5: Method and Tool 3: The Cube Service Value (CSV).
Chapter 6: How to apply the TVF? A six-step approach to territorial development.
Chapter 7: Three case studies to put the TVF Method to test.

The first two chapters are conceptual and allow readers to understand the key concepts underlying the implementation of this Framework. They emphasize the importance of service marketing in the construction of territorial policies.

Chapter 1 defines the existing places and interactions between governance and regulation in the context of the development of territorial policies. It develops the different institutional dimensions that are at the origin of a territorial dynamic and presents how they interact. The reference to the three levels of institutionalization of the territory offers the first modality for the construction of territorial policies. The articulation of these three levels allows revisiting the concepts of Bottom-up and Top-down and redefining governance and regulation as well as their relationships in a new perspective on the dynamic of local development.

The following chapter, Chapter 2, introduces the issue of value creation and its attractiveness for the beneficiaries of development offers. The attractiveness offers direct links to its acceptability by the beneficiary stakeholders. The influence of this offer proposition as a vector for development is essential for understanding the general dynamic of development. The chapter is particularly interested in the characteristics of the offer propositions contained in a development plan. Service theory provides the conceptual framework in which the conditions of attractiveness and acceptability of these propositions are set. Values and, in particular, values in use, in exchange and potential values are introduced by the TVF as the privileged objects to master to create a dynamic of development based on their attractiveness.

The next three chapters offer a methodology based on three tools for analysis and action. The complementarity of these three tools allows structuring a complete process for implementing a diagnosis or a territorial development policy. It presents all of the dynamics of territorial development as, relatively, a configuration of resolved tensions among the stakeholders. These tensions are at work in governance as the organization of decisions between actors and regulation as the organization of technical solutions that concretize decisions. They are present between the legal or normative Top-down and the Bottom-up of local or even individual initiatives. From the analysis of the resolution modes of these tensions, Chapter 3 proposes to the analysts a typology of nine modes of governance and regulation presenting for each their relatively optimal contribution to the general dynamics of territorial development. This typology serves as a basis for understanding different types of territorial functioning, identifies dysfunctions and reveals the possible ways of intervention.

The analysis of stakeholders, development actors, is an essential factor in the success of a territorial project. Chapter 4 mainly deals with stakeholders including beneficiaries of development offers. It offers a tool for analyzing and understanding the behavior of stakeholders. Besides merely identifying them, this chapter analyzes their positions in terms of power, legitimacy and urgency in the process of implementing development. These three terms allow to assess the stakeholders' places and roles in the configuration of the tensions presented in the previous chapter. This assessment applies to methods of resolving tensions arising from relationships between stakeholders and their negotiating capacity. A typology proposes four types of general dynamics of territorial development to favor the synthesis of these assessments.

Chapter 5 deals with value creation. It is central to the TVF both by the nature of the value and by its methods of creation in the offer propositions. A diagnostic and innovation method is presented to deal concretely with the attractiveness of the territorial development offers, propositions, existing or incoming. The Cube Service Value (CSV) aims to improve quality and innovation in the development offers. It also seeks concrete solutions that reduce tensions among the concerned stakeholders and reinforce the general dynamic of the development of a territory. The CSV helps to design offer propositions that promote development. It interprets regulation as a phase of combining and transforming resources between providers and beneficiaries. In this combination, the beneficiary is in a position to co-produce, and even to co-create or transfer value. The regulation associated with an adapted governance system, the engine of development, can make the beneficiary an actor of the value creation and participation, such as, in governance.

As a diagnostic and prospective tool, the CSV allows assessing the contribution of existing or future offers.

The last two chapters are devoted to testing the TVF. A complete step-by-step methodology builds the diagnosis of the territorial development dynamics. It gives access to successive syntheses to orient future actions based on the findings of a given development situation. This methodology is detailed in Chapter 6. It is structured in six steps where the analysts and the policymakers can find, for each of them, a series of questions that guide the diagnostic process. At the end of the sixth step, the key questions of the situation of a territory from the point of view of its development, its general dynamics and the possible ways of its optimization find an answer to act.

The last chapter, Chapter 7, presents three applications of the proposed methods. These case studies show, in three different contexts, how a choice of identical development theme can lead to energize a series of other development themes and open up prospects for boosting progress in the longer term. The TVF places these perspectives in the modes of value creation likely to reduce the configuration of tensions that the method identifies.

The VALUES Program (Value Analysis of Local Utilities of Enterprises from Social Sector) was a research program registered in the European research program: SEVENTH FRAMEWORK PROGRAMME, Marie Curie Actions People, International Research Staff Exchange Scheme.

The VALUES research program was focused on a central theme relating governance and regulation of the sector of the social economy in a territorial context. This project was based on Vaesken and Zafiropoulou (2008) model centered to social innovation resulting from the articulation between modes of governance and modes of regulation.

The program treated three specific research orientations of social policies and local development:

1. Cultural policies (cultural management, place of users in the construction of cultural policies, innovating systems and devices). This axis points the difficulty in taking into account the requests of stakeholders in the construction of cultural policies building oriented to social regulation.

2. Healthcare policies (centered on active participation of users, innovating systems and devices of management in isolated territories). This axis analyzes news relationships, partnerships and services characterizing the healthcare sector, having for goal to manage medical territories.

3. Policies of social and economic integration of disadvantaged populations (innovating systems and devices of management). Within the framework of the social and professional integration, it is important to study the roles of private and public operators in order to specify different types of configurations. These configurations aim to answer problems of social and economic insertion.

Moreover, a transverse axis on home care and integrated services was developed.

This multidisciplinary research project has integrated both economic, public policies and public management approaches.

• To share university knowledge in the fields of social economy applied to partners territories.

• To cross research on regulation practices integrated in social policies.

• To analyze the role of users and to identify the strategies of actors.

• To describe territorial specificities and to theorize managerial practices.

The program has been undertaken for 4 years from 2012 to 2016. VALUES mobilized universities and high school, three countries, 15 researchers and 5 research teams.

- Université des sciences et technologies de Lille1 – Lille, France

- Université Mohamed V – Souissi, Morocco

- Universitatea Lucian Blaga din Sibiu, Romania

- SKEMA Business School, Lille, France

Chapter 1

Governance, Regulation and Territorial Policies

This chapter lays the foundations that serve as theoretical references to the construction of the Territorial Values Framework (henceforth, TVF) presented in Chapter 3. These references draw from all theoretical efforts that make the territory a privileged area of renewed public action. They endeavor to define a framework for territorial policy and some implementation principles for its action and development plan.

The territory is defined by all social, economic and cultural relationships in a space regarded as a strategic territory. A territorial policy defines a "territorial project" which integrates the territorial identity and the objectives of the action plan. The implementation of a territorial strategy depends necessarily on its organizational modes.

A territorial organization seeks, more particularly, to intensify the interactions and partnerships among different public institutions and different partners. It tries to build new links between the actors in or out of the territory. These relationships must specifically favor the encounter between territorial visions, i.e., internal to the territory and the external actors who interact in the territory. This results in action strategies that are neither categorical nor sectoral but said to be appropriate (territorialized policy).

The territory thus offers a specific framework of intervention which takes charge of all the problems which arise in a given territory. It thus carries out a partnership action, associating different actors present or not in the territory, adapted to each local situation as defined by the configuration of the territory or territories.

This chapter firstly discusses several useful concepts for understanding the articulation of territorial policies as well as their meaning and institutional complexity. In the second step, the methods of territorial intervention (regulation) are analyzed by linking them to the actors' operating modes (governance). Finally, the logic between national action and local approach is defined to capture the multiplicity and different interactions in a territorial development approach.

1.1 The territory: a fact, a construct or an experience?

The concept of "territory" is a controversial concept which refers to different frameworks of analysis. In the field of social sciences (geography, sociology, management and political economy) there is a clear consensus on the necessarily constructed character of the territory. Thus this concept does not focus simply on the logic of zone or assignment space, but takes on a more global and dynamic meaning: the factual territory gives way to a construction dynamic of a lived space. This concept is therefore enriched by the different approaches offered by the social sciences.

The term territory only appears in the economic literature with Marshall (1890) and, more recently, with Perroux (1950). It is far from being recognized by all economists as an important explanatory variable.

The territory has often been the subject of systematic rejections on the pretext that if it adds to the realism of the models, it would in no way contribute to the understanding of economic phenomena.

However, the development of spatial analysis and models of the location of firms such as the models of Von Thünen (1926), Isard (1954) and those of geographic economics (Krugman 1995, Arthur 1995), show the growing importance of spatial analysis in economics. Spatial analysis retains only the broader notion of physical space of the territory. A large number of authors in economics tend to leave classic sectoral analysis to orient their research towards a territorial approach (Marshall 1890, Perroux 1950).

The lineage of these economists is found in the various schools of thought in the area of territorial development. The principle of local production systems finds a strong territorial root with multiple theoretical orientations.

The territory is often the starting point for developments that differ in orientation without being contradictory. This is how the theory of industrial or innovative districts (Becatini 1979 Marshall 1890) was a huge success with authors like Courlet, Pecqueur and Soulage (1993) (development of the Arve valley from the small parts turning industry, or of the shoe industry in Cholet, France).

The concept of proximity in the construction of the territory becomes essential, beyond just geography. Territorial economists are interested in the fact that territorial proximity is constructed from three types of proximity:

- Organizational proximity: It concerns interindividual and collective relations within organizations and between organizations. It also incorporates the relational proximity between the actors and stakeholders of the territory.

- Geographical proximity: It takes into account the physical characteristics (geography of space) or those linked to the facilities. Scale can be spatial or economic.

- Institutional Proximity: It is based on history, organizational processes ... it emphasizes the feeling of belonging.

Territorial proximity is at the intersection of these different proximities.

For researchers, some of them, members of the GREMI (European Research Group on Innovative Environments), territorial development is essentially the result of a process of innovation (Maillat 1992, Quevit 1991, Perrin 1990, 1992, Aydalot 1986). As it is the case, for example, with Silicon Valley (Chong-Moon et al. 2000). Other authors (Leborgne, Lipietz, 1988) have mainly approached territorial evolution in a post-Fordist current. In these different currents, the origins of territorial development are multiple and add up. The approach to this development remains essentially geographic. It analyzes a dynamic based on the territorial structuring of companies as actors without yet reference to the notion of local development.

The approach to the territory from the actors introduces the vision of sociologists. The territory is perceived as an element structuring the games of actors. Thus, sociologists like Ganne (1991) go beyond the definition of the company, as a simple production structure, in localized industrial systems, to emphasize their function of organizing the territory: the optimal valuation of the resources carried out by the company also goes beyond the economic plan, leading to take into account in another way the other factors constituting its environment, or rather the different ways in which the company builds and organizes it (Ganne 1991). The organization of the territory by a system of actors, in which the company is an important, even fundamental, link is also underlined by Thoenig (1993) when he presents the (local) territory from the angle of the sociology of organizations. According to him, the local, as a specific territorial entity, becomes an autonomous actor participating in an overall collective regulation, alongside the central which is itself an actor among others in decisions or choices (Thoenig 1993).

It is necessary to be interested in the geographers' vision of the territory. The first approach is undoubtedly that of Vidal de la Blache (1905). The "territory" is perceived as an element of regional analysis, resulting from the entanglement of natural data and human influences throughout history. In this sense, for the geographers, the territory is not an abstract space ... but a concrete space whose physical and historical characteristics should not be ignored (Giblin Delvallet 1993). Fremont completes this definition by specifying that, for geographers, it is the notion of "lived space" that becomes fundamental. The lived space (Fremont 1976) designates the control that each actor has of his environment. The economist Perroux (1961) proposes a notion close to that of lived space with the concept of polarized space, in his theory of the polarization of productive activities. According to this author, men have the power to create their space of influence and action.

In short, the territory is a real construct in perpetual dynamics and evolution. It follows from this definition that the territory has several components:

- Geographical territory: It is a portion of space-delimited by physical and climatic elements, such for example: mountain, river, desert, arid, semi-arid territory, plain and littoral.

- Institutional territory: It is the result of an administrative division. It corresponds to a sub-national level represented, among others, by the municipality, county or region which are both administrative districts of the State and local communities.

- Cognitive territory (identity): It is defined as a space with which the population identifies according to cultural proximity, customs, traditions, language, common history and sense of belonging.

- The project area: This is a territory defined according to a specific action to help it develop through the intervention of the state and local authorities.

This territory can also be defined as the relevant territory according to a specific area, for example, a tourist region that deserved to be valued and developed. The relevant territory integrates the four components described above and takes into account:

- The economic dimension (resource)

- The appropriate level that favors the action of territorial development actors.

- The critical size that encourages a particular organization.

- The proximity which facilitates the implementation and realization of projects.

This relevant territory constitutes the operational base of the various actions and approaches of territorial development. It is at the origin of a political (political territory) and managerial framework for intervention. The implementation of a territory management approach necessarily involves the construction of a territorial policy:

- Its framework is defined by all the social relations delimited in a space: the "Strategic territory".

- Its meaning is characterized by its project (territorial project) through the definition of the identity of a territory and the objectives of the resulting action in a "Territory strategy".

- Its operational variation is based on the relationships and interactions between the various public institutions and the various partners involved in a "Territorial action strategy" (neither categorical nor sectoral).

The territory-based approach in the definition and conduct of public policies facilitates the implementation of transversal actions taking charge of all the dimensions of the problems to be dealt with as they combine in a given territory. It is a partnership action which brings together the various actors present in the territory and which adapts to the local situation as defined by the configuration of the territory.

Thus, the territorial strategy sets itself as a collective action designating local spaces but also a multiplicity of perimeters inducing overlaps. It is a construction of localized representation and tangles of interests. The territorial strategy fits into a more global (extraterritorial) dimension which obliges decision-makers to "think global to act local and think local to act global".

1.2 The complementarity of territorial policies

To understand the complementarity of local, regional and national actions in a territory, an institutional framework for territorial analysis is required. The adoption and adaptation of this framework underline the existing complementarities between territorial policies inspired by external actors and territorialized policies under the responsibility of the territory actors themselves.

1.2.1 Territorial institutions and policies

Territorial policies are an essential part of an institutional context. They are directly pertained to the operation of public and private organizations that participate in the construction and development of territorial policies. This operation is subject to institutional analysis. It examines the influences of the environment on organizations. It considers that the search for optimal efficiency (DiMaggio and Powel 1983, Meyer and Rowan 1977) notably involves cultural and symbolic norms (Leca 2006, Huault 2009) in terms of institutional constraints and pressures. As a result, Scott (2001) specifies that institutions can be defined as structures and uses that give meanings and stability to the social behaviors of agents included in the territory.

Institutional analysis refers to three frameworks that can be complementary or developed in isolation: the legislative framework, the normative framework and the cultural and cognitive framework (Scott 2001, DiMaggio and Powell 1991).

The following table matches these three frameworks (Brunel and Triki 2009).

Table 1-1: Comparative approach of frameworks

	Initiator	**Method**	**Approach**	**Stakeholders**
Legislative framework	State or institutions defining laws and rules	Coercive: rules and laws	Apply to every one	Institutions and lobbies
Normative framework	Standardization and management agencies	Initiative: freedom of agreement	Agreement on standards	Voluntary stakeholders
Cultural and cognitive framework	Society	Apply to uses and practices	Self imposed	Social evolutions vision

In the legislative framework, relations among the actors are often perceived to be a power struggle in favor of the state that imposes its rules. This approach, stemming from the theories of "Public Choice" (Buchanan and Tullock 1962, Mueller 1980, 1989, 1997), can lead to acutely bureaucratic visions (Galbraith 1967, Weber 1919), giving way to a rise in the power of the technostructure which imposes its rules. Bureaucracy limits initiatives and leads to regulated behavior of actors (Simon 1957) through clearly enacted procedures and rules. It is, therefore, a very instrumental approach to territorial policies.

In the normative framework, these values dictate the modes of society function in a given territory. It is fundamentally based on the principles of Durkheim (1893) and Person (1952), who state that individual motivation relies more on shared values as long as these standards are inscribed in an institutional environment. The normative framework gives rise to the development of the theory on stakeholders (Freeman 1984), and its various evolutions (Donaldson 1995, Carroll 1996, Rowley 1997, Mitchell, Agle and Wood 1997, Henriques and Sadorsky 1999, Beaulieu et al. 2002, Bryson 2004, Bourne 2005, Olander and Landin 2005, Ackermann and Eden 2010, Jeffery 2009, Parmar 2010, Bourne and Walker 2005, Postema et al. 2012) which highlight the games and issues of actors at the origin of these standards definitions.

The institutional analysis of the territory in the cognitive and cultural framework examines society in the form of shared individual practices (tradition, ways of thinking, etc.) (Tolbert and Ucker 1996), or in the form of collective actions. Institutions pursue to decrease the unpredictability of social behavior and seek to impose constraints that are sanctioned either by the social context and other agents or by the legal context (Scoot 2001).

Finally, the cultural framework is based on the mental representations of each actor. It leads to the construction of common rules accepted and recognized by all. It is an approach to territorial policies where Top-down is not imposed but leaves rooms for the autonomous development of the territory. It is a long-term construction, considering different individual and collective criteria that must be taken into account in the process of defining territorial policies.

1.2.2 Territories and territorial policies

The construction of territorial policies is, therefore, of a combinatory nature from the three frameworks of institutional analysis shown above. The first considers the production or frame of public action standards within the legal framework. It is an operational mode that relies on the ability of territorial managers to legislate, taking into account the operating conditions of territories (economic, functional, social, etc.). It considers an exercise of the law in expediency and consent.

The second framework develops the methods of management and government in order to govern the territory. This framework becomes the benchmark for local management where each territorial entity (municipality, etc.) has specific skills (management of proximity problems, redistribution agent or multiplier actor). It is a normative framework that binds on all territorial entities.

The third framework selects perceptions, practices and social behaviors without explicit reference to the two previous frameworks. These individual and collective behaviors guide the economic and social realities of the territory. They define a cultural framework where development takes on a social character (the citizenship of the participants and their ability to negotiate new collective relations with the institutions) and a territorial character (a combination of economic, social and cultural operations).

It is through the combination of these three frameworks that collective actions are interpreted and born. They are built on the multiplicity of territorial policies inducing Top-down and Bottom-up overlaps. This approach allows it to adapt policies to the specificities of territories while maintaining overall consistency, enhancement and readability of territorial policies and a move towards a partnership approach.

1.3 Territorial regulation and governance

1.3.1 The articulation of the three frameworks of institutional analysis

Territorial development brings together the three frameworks of institutional analysis (see above). For the legislative framework, it is the principle of the universality of the law that binds on all territorial nationals according to a top-down approach. The decisions taken in this context are "binding" and imposing a set of rules that apply universally to the entire population concerned. In this context, what is considered is the relationship between individual interest and collective interest. The universalism advocated by this model responds to the practice of the common interest stemming from the definition of laws and regulations.

Through the actors, their roles and systems of representations, their places and modes of relationship, territorial development also favors normative approaches. They ensure the articulation between the bottom and the top, and between the ascendant and the descendant. It is also true for cognitive and cultural approaches. The principle of territorial governance then becomes a management mode combining these different registers (for example, taking into account the results of citizen consultations in the definition of territorial policies). In Chapter 3, governance also incorporates another form of combination that of all the stakeholders involved in the realization of territorial offers and the uses they deliver. According to Stoker (1998), "Governance involves a complex set of actors and institutions that do not all belong to the sphere of government. It reflects interdependence between the powers and the institutions associated with collective action."

Governance involves the networks of autonomous actors and assumes that it is possible to act without necessary reliance on the power of the state. Territorial governance is considered a process of permanent negotiation and persuasion among extremely heterogeneous actors. The actors are involved in territorial policies in order to make the three frameworks of institutional analysis compatible for actors geographically close, with a view to the realization of a territorial project (Gilly and Perrat 2003): defining orientations, allocating resources, implementing methods and evaluating their effects (Vaesken 2014). It is built around actors who share a common vision or who are able to act on this vision. Gumuchian (2007) qualifies this type of actors as territorialized actors. Actors who take place in a territorialized environment (Vaesken 1996) as a space built by the actors themselves and as a place for collective action.

Governance, in this case, can only be said as "sited" (Vaesken et al. 2008a and b; Vaesken 2014; Zaoual 2004; Maby 2008), in the sense that it accounts for a shared territorial dimension and is defined by all the actors concerned. In the context of territorial governance, the area of action, i.e., its site, is the area of development and the location of the intervention that involves the three institutional frameworks. This governance then takes into account all of the economic, political and social dimensions and induces a will to work in a spirit of synergy and mutual trust (Aghaï and Vaesken 2010).

1.3.2 Towards new modes of territorial intervention

The actual articulation of the three frameworks of institutional analysis forms the basis of territorial regulation. It describes a dynamic process of territorial development management. This process is relayed by a system of territorial governance associating the multiplicity of actors implicated in the definition and the implementation of territorial policies and collective projects. This articulation creates new modes of intervention for public action, calling into question traditional centralized and Top-down models (Holec and Brunet-Jolivad 2000, Leloup, Moyard and Pecqueur 2005).

Territorial governance thus describes the game of localized compromises and power relations (Gilly and Perrat 2003), the processes of negotiation and arbitration, allowing the multiple forms of regulation. These have already been analyzed by Gilly and Pecqueur (1995), and Zaoual (2008). The regulatory approach generally requires a reference environment. This environment can be local, regional, national (mainstream of the public economy and economic school of regulation) or global.

In this classic conception of territorial policies, regulatory practices often combine global regulation, of the Top-down type in the sense of economic trends (Agglietta 1976, Boyer 1996, 2003, Boyer and Saillard 1995), of the economy public (Laffont 1998) and social regulation, and of the bottom-up type (Reynaud 1997, 1988, De Terssac 2003, Crozier and Friedberg 1977, Brechet 2008). Galbraith and Weber show that a system of imposing rules in a "Top-down" way, even if they are negotiated, leads to the development of a bureaucratic model with perverse effects (Galbraith 1967, Weber 1919). The integration of a "Bottom-up" vision, based on cultural and cognitive bases, completes a Top-down approach with a Bottom-up approach, stemming from civil society.

1.3.3 The Territorial Values Framework (TVF): building a reading grid

The first component of the TVF: a regulation typology

Territorial regulation is defined as a process of making territorial offers based on available resources. It depends on two criteria. One is the Capacity of autonomy left to territorial stakeholders, providers and beneficiaries, in the combination of available resources. If the capacity is weak, it means that suppliers are limited in their proposals and in their ability to combine resources and make them attractive. Likewise, this means that the beneficiaries are also limited in their choice of offers and in the way they can combine their resources with those of the providers. This criterion reflects the level of all the stakeholders' initiatives. The other depends on the rules that govern the actions of territorial actors and the availability of resources, whether imposed or come from their own initiative.

Table 1-2: Typology of territorial regulation

	Capacity of autonomy left to territorial stakeholders	
Weight of the Rules which govern the actions of territorial stakeholders	**Weak**	**Strong**
Weak	Case 1: Territories « let on its own » Emergent Regulation	Case 3: Territories led by the stakeholders' initiatives Autonomous Regulation
Strong	Case 2: Dependent Territories Centralized Regulation	Case 4: Agile territories Sited Regulation

Four situations are illustrated as above.

Case 1, presenting the territories "let on its own", underlines the possible existence of territories that have no real stakes. These territories have little capacity for actions, which is particularly explained by a weakness of available resources.

With regard to case 2, the "dependent territories", the territorial actions are strongly controlled. The control applies to the rules that govern territorial actions. It is based on a hierarchical function of the territories.

For case 3, the territorial stakeholders benefit from a strong capacity for autonomy. In this case, we can consider that the regulation is of autonomous type. This can lead to a form of territorial empowerment and can be a source of territorial inequality.

Case 4 refers to the strong autonomy of territorial stakeholders. This can result in the implementation of real endogenous development projects. However, this development remains framed by a system of rules.

The second component of the TVF: Practices of territorial governance

The practice of local development relates the regulation modes to the types of governance that exist in a territory. These modes of governance are the systems of actors that interact to build the rules in which territorial regulation is organized (Friedberg 1993). In this context, the development approach leads to the inclusion of local democracy as a basis for discussion and negotiation between the various actors and the territorial institutions.

The dynamics, interactions and institutional processes among actors, constitute the hardcore of territorial governance (Vaesken 2011). However, the governance of territories is not only a fact limited to the territory itself. The stakeholders are both specific actors who are involved in the management of the territory and actors who are not directly linked to the territory. The latter may belong to institutional structures which act on themes (employment, culture, etc.) covering other territories. These thematic and territorial overlays organize the various dimensions of local development. It is therefore advisable to consider a system of multi-governance, or a plurality of governance modes, which is organized within a territory (Enjolras 2001, 2005) in articulation with extraterritorial modes of governance (territories which develop a relationship of influence with the territory concerned). It is through these successive interactions that rules of operation and cooperation among actors within the territory (Weick 1969) are structured.

This multi-governance crosses two modes of governance: territorial governance and extraterritorial governance. Both are based on an emerging or structured level of organization. Governance is emerging when a set of actors and institutions spontaneously organize themselves to manage an initiative. And it is structured when it is guided by the classic operating rules of a territory.

The table 1-3 demonstrates multi-governance which presents a holistic vision of territorial governance. It highlights the coexistence of different governance types, ranging from emerging governance to so-called "sited" governance. Between these two types of governance, the more specific types of organizing governance are placed according to Bottom-up or Top-down methods. Multi-governance consists of new institutional configurations that define the modalities of coordination between different categories of actors involved in territorial governance. These configurations correspond to four types of governance.

Table 1-3: Typology of territorial governance practices

		Extra territorial Governance	
		Emergent Approach	Structured Approach
Territorial Governance	Emergent Approach	Type 1: Emerging governance based on initiatives to be developed Emergent Governance	Type 3: Joint governance based on an extraterritorial accompaniment of territorial initiatives Top-down joint Governance
	Structured Approach	Type 2: Good territorial practices taken into account in an extraterritorial framework Bottom-up joint Governance	Type 4: Ensuring consistency of extraterritorial and territorial modes of governance sited governance

Type 1 presents the emerging governance. It integrates the actors in an informal process of concretization of initiatives that are built progressively. They are generally specific partnerships targeting emerging and innovative actions or projects, in the sense that they do not exist beforehand. This type of governance is important to be included in a territorial governance approach because it is a force for proposal and innovation. It can combine local and external actors in the development of the emerging project.

Type 2, the bottom-up joint governance, presents a territorial project for which the state supports along specific lines and themes. It is institutional governance, often formal and plural, which implies the global nature of local actors in a global vision of the territory. The partnership dimension between the state and the territory is necessary. The state supports local development to be consistent with the directions of national policies. This type of governance gives rise to thematic contracts concerning a global project.

Type 3 presents the top-down joint governance in which the national dimension and priorities prevail over the regional dimension. The resulting partnership is formal and institutional. It translates into local support for national policies. Concretely, it is a local variation of national development and spatial planning schemes. They impose themselves on the territories and require a real involvement of local authorities and institutional actors.

Finally, type 4 characterizes a formal and institutionalized partnership of the pluralist type. It is the framework for "sited" governance located in the territories. It mainly involves public actors in negotiating the nature of public interventions and resorting to technocracy for their implementation (Enjolras 2005).

Territorial governance, therefore, corresponds, by definition, to a partnership organization that involves local actors, ranging from citizens to institutions through the private sector. Depending on this organization, different types of regulation appear. Each of them involves a system of negotiation and collaboration to seek in the dialogue between territorial and extra-territorial actors.

The territorial dynamics: the inseparability of Governance and Regulation

The TVF states that understanding all territorial dynamics requires the inseparable nature of the game between governance and regulation. In this game, the practice of territorial governance articulates bottom-up and top-down initiatives. It organizes intermediation to facilitate this articulation. As for the regulation, it sets up the practices that lead to the territorial propositions of the action plan from the support and mediation mechanisms between the mobilized actors (Boyer and Saillard 1995, Gilly and Pecqueur 1995). Two components are then to be analyzed. One is the nature, place and role of actors and mechanisms for stimulating, concerted action, decision-making and operationalization. The other is the processes for defining territorial offers, translating them into priority actions and implementing them.

The following table relates the types of governance and regulation to the approaches for territorial development, from an emerging approach to a sited approach.

Table 1-4: Characteristics of territorial governance and regulation

	Territorial dynamics in the two dimensions taken into account by territorial action	
	Governance	*Regulation*
Emergent approach (located)	Organization between local actors to promote consultation, decision-making, monitoring and evaluation	Consensual and tacit development and implementation of practices
Sited approach	Means implemented to support information, stakeholders' consultation	Institutionalization of practices based on procedures and predefined rules

1.4 Revisiting territorial policies: the TVF Governance regulation interactions chart

The interactions between regulation and governance enable to understand the foundations of a revisited territorial policy and to introduce the approach of the TVF. To understand the dynamics that are specific to the implementation of a territorial policy, it is crucial to reveal the possible states of their interdependence across the approaches of governance and those of regulation. The intersection of the actors' descending wills and those ascending ones also promote a good understanding of the negotiating powers at stake and the objectives in terms of their evolution. These two associated and crossing forms develop a dynamic that ensures the adaptation of the territory to its internal and external environment and provides precious indications to how to guarantee its development. These crossings should enable to stress different scenarios that exist in the context of the construction of territorial policies. It remains a question of whether building a frame of reference that starts from the crossing of regulation and governance and that of bottom-up and top-down clearly reveals four types of territorial policies. These are complementary and not mutually exclusive and can ensure a better understanding of territorial dynamics.

Employing these crossings makes it possible to read the positioning that characterizes the given situation of a territory and to reveal its most suitable development prospects. The development of territory must question the ways of its evolution regarding the general repository of territorial policies. This analysis serves as the basis for an approach to building a policy that is best suited to the territory, including a broad vision of all the opportunities available for its development.

Through these crossings and the four proposed territorial situations, policymakers can rely on a given state or initial situation of the territory, and combine these different types to predict and energize its development. This construction offers the points of analysis helping to define the situation to be reached (desired final situation of the territory). The transition from one state to another will be characteristic of an approach to a territorial development project. To achieve these intersections, governance and regulation are vectored, according to the principle of a continuum spanning from an emerging situation towards a sited approach. The chart thus creates forms the basis of a territorial diagnosis.

Figure 1-1: The TVF Governance Regulation interactions chart

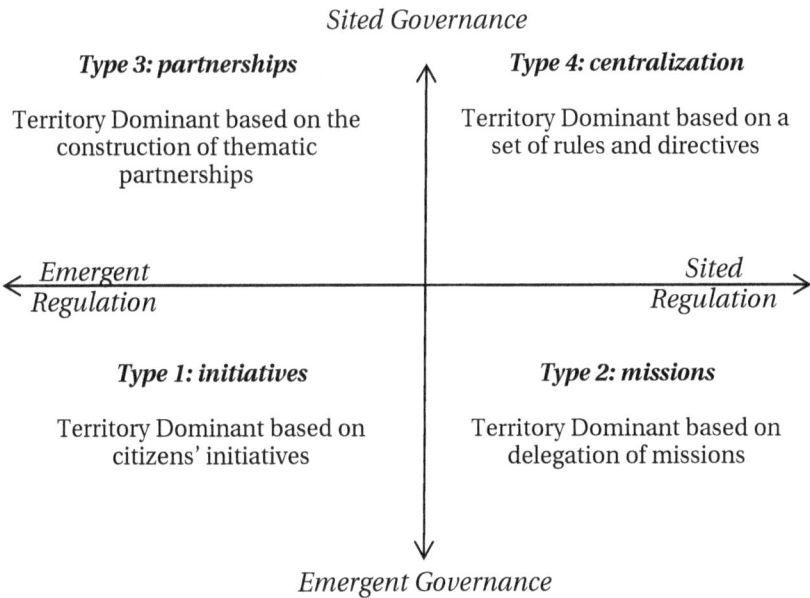

Sited Governance

Type 3: partnerships

Territory Dominant based on the construction of thematic partnerships

Type 4: centralization

Territory Dominant based on a set of rules and directives

Emergent Regulation ←

→ *Sited Regulation*

Type 1: initiatives

Territory Dominant based on citizens' initiatives

Type 2: missions

Territory Dominant based on delegation of missions

Emergent Governance

From these crossings, this chart emphasizes the four main types of operation in a territory and put forward a real logic of action.

Type 1: Initiatives; represents a situation of widespread initiative. It is characteristic of a situation of emerged governance and emerged regulation.

Type 2: Missions; highlights the result of the crossing between a sited regulation and an emerged governance. The rules and directives serve as a reference to action.

Type 3: Partnership; points out territories in a partnership framework between the actors of a thematic sector and institutional authorities. Interventions are not specified by policy choices, but are the subject of an organization among actors according to principles of organized proximity. In this context, the roles and functions of stakeholders are essential.

Type 4: Centralized; is the organizational mode adopted by central decision-makers in the territorial field. The local government carries out institutional production and the structuring of standards is considerably centralized and based on a high degree of confidence in the governance structure.

Governance and regulation evolve along with territorial and extraterritorial contributions according to the strategic directions of the action plans. The actors' role of the territorial action is to propose modes of governance that reinforce the impacts of regulation. The actors perform their influence and are subject to context effects.

Table 1-5: Logics of territorial policies construction

	Systems of Actors	*Processes*	*Projects*
Type 1 *Initiatives*	Emerging and *ad-hoc*, not necessarily pre-existing in the territory	Informal, emerging and *ad-hoc*. The processes are structured specifically to ensure the intervention and generally stay at the local level	Specific and innovative and emerging type
Type 2 *Missions*	Structured globally around the intervention theme and organized by mission	Structured and articulated with institutional actors, but informal	Innovative but part of a specific intervention framework (delegation of the central approach)
Type 3 *Partnerships*	Network and thematic type	Formal, organized and structured which can be territorial or extra territorial	Projects that define the thematic orientations of future interventions
Type 4 *Centralization*	Political and institutional	Formal, institutional and contractual	Structuring projects with an institutional dimension

Their influence and ability to influence depends on the territory and the types of projects. The territory occupies a central place in the balance of governance and the regulation of territorial interventions. Regarding the construction of the territorial policy, the framework proposed in this Chapter1 focuses on the position of operators and decision-makers.

The territorial approach of action plans based on this logic of interactions among the different elements, as described above, leads to the construction of a territorial analysis and development tool that will be presented in Chapter 3. This tool, supplemented by two others in Chapters 4 and 5, tends to help to revisit territorial policies by taking into account all the places and roles defined by all the stakeholders in the action plans. The following Chapter 2 develops one of the essential components of this revisit concerning these stakeholders: the component of the beneficiaries of the action plan and the offers subject to their acceptance, their judgment of satisfaction and the contribution to their participative transformation. The analysis in this revisit of the place and role of the beneficiaries of the territorial offer necessarily introduces the theme of the value propositions contained in these offers.

This consideration refers to one of the key issues of territorial development: the inseparable character of the successful territorial development policies and the capacity of influence of policymakers. This influence is present in the territorial offers through their value propositions to the beneficiaries. As a driver of the territorial development, the influence depends on the success of these propositions to beneficiary citizens thanks to the attractiveness of the values they contain. In the TVF, the beneficiaries take a full place and role in territorial governance and participate according to the concepts presented in Chapter 2 in the production of the territorial offer, based on a regulation approach where the question of success by the influence and attractiveness of offers dominates.

Bibliography

Ackermann, F. and Eden, C. 2010. "Strategic management of stakeholders: theory and practice." *Long Range Planning* 44, 3: pp.179-196.

Aghaï, A. and Vaesken, P. 2010. "Synergie et solidarité d'acteurs en zone rurale. Une approche de la rationalité et de la gouvernance située dans le contexte d'un douar marocain." In *Gérer les ressources humaines en Afrique*, edited by EMS Management et Société, collection: Questions de société.

Aglietta, M. 1976. *Régulation et crise du capitalisme*. Paris: Calmann-Levy.

Aydalot, Ph. 1986. *Milieux innovateurs en Europe*. Paris: GREMI.

Beaulieu, S. and Pasquero, J. 2002. "Reintroducing Stakeholder Dynamics in Stakeholder Thinking: a Negotiated Order Perspective." In *Unfolding Stakeholder Thinking: Theory, Responsibility and Engagement*, edited by Andriof J, Waddock S, Sutherland Rahman S, Husted B. Sheffield, 101-118. UK: Greenleaf Publishing.

Becatini, G. 1979. "Dal settore industriale al distretto industriale, *Rivista di Economia e Politica Industriale*." 2: pp. 7-21.

Bourne, L. 2005. "Project relationship management and the Stakeholder Circle." PhD Dissertation. http://www.mosaicprojects.com.au/PDF_Papers/P021_L_Bourne_Thesis.pdf

Bourne, L. and Walker, D. H. T. 2005. "Visualizing and mapping stakeholder influence." *Management Decision* 43, 5: pp. 649-660.

Boyer, R. 2003. "Les institutions dans la théorie de la régulation." *CEPREMAP-ENS, CNRS, EHESS*, n°8.

Boyer, R. 1986. *Théorie de la Régulation: une analyse critique*. Paris: La Découverte.

Boyer, Y. and Saillard, Y. 1995. *Théorie de la régulation. L'état des savoirs*, Paris: La Découverte.

Bréchet, J.P. 2008. "Le regard de la théorie de la régulation sociale de Jean-Daniel Reynaud" *Revue Française de gestion* 184: pp. 13-34.

Brunel, M. and Triki, D. 2008. *Peut-on standardiser la RSE? Une approche théorique*. Pau: ESC.

Bryson, J. M. 2004. "What to do when stakeholders matter: stakeholder identification and analysis techniques." *Public Management Review* 6, 1: pp. 21-53.

Buchanan, J. Tullock, C. 1962. *The Calculus of Concent*. Ann Arbor: University of Michigan Press.

Carroll, A.B. 1996. *Business and society: ethic and stakeholder management*. Cincinnati, South-Western Publishing, 3rd Edition.

Courlet, C. Pecqueur, B. and Soulage, B. 1993. "Industrie et dynamiques de territoires», *RERU* 3.

Crozier, M and Friedberg, E. 1977. *"L'acteur et le système: Les contraintes de l'action collective"*. Collection Sociologie Politique.

De Terssac, G. 2003. *La théorie de la régulation sociale de J.D. Reynaud*. Paris: La découverte.

DiMaggio, P.J. and Powell, W.W. 1991. *The New Institutionalism in Organizational Analysis*. Chicago: University of Chicago Press.

Donaldson, T. and Preston, L. E. 1995. The Stakeholder Theory of the Corporation: Concepts, Evidence, and Implications. *The Academy of Management Review*. 20,1: pp. 65-91.

Durkheim, E. 1983. *De la division du travail social*. Paris: PUF 2007.

Enjolras, B. 2001. "Coordination failure, property rights and nonprofits organization." *Anal of public and cooperative economics* 4.

Enjolras B. 2005. "Economie Sociale et solidaire et régimes de gouvernance.» *RECMA* 296.

Freeman, R. Edward,1984. *Strategic Management: A stakeholder approach*. Boston: Pitman.

Fremont, A. 1976. *La région, espace vécu*. Paris: PUF.

Galbraith, J. K. 1967. *Le Nouvel Etat Industriel*. Paris, Gallimard.

Ganne, B. 1991. "Les approches du local et des systèmes industriels locaux". *Sociologie du travail* 4, 91.

Giblin-Delvallet, B. 1993. "La géographie et l'analyse du local: le retour vers le politique", in *A la recherche du local*, edited by A. Mabileau, Logiques économiques. Paris: L'harmattan.

Gilly, J.P. and Pecqueur, B. 1995. "La dimension locale de la régulation." In *Théorie de la régulation: l'état des savoirs*, edited by R. Boyer and Y. Saillard Y, Coll. Recherches. Paris: La Découverte.

Gilly, J.P. and Perrat, J. 2002. "Développement local et coopération décentralisée, entre régulation locale et régulation globale." *Colloque économie Méditerranéenne Monde Arabe*, Sousse, Septembre.

Gumuchian, H. 2007. "Le concept d'acteur territorialisé: action/discours/ intentions." In *Apport de l'approche territoriale à l'économie du développement*, edited by J. Lapèze. Paris: L'Harmattan, coll. Economie Critique.

Henriques, I. and Sariorsky P. 1999. "The relationship between environmental commitment and managerial importance of stakeholder importance." *Academy of Management Journal* 204: pp. 479-485.

Holec, N. and Brunet-Jolivad, G. 2000. "De la gouvernance des économies à celle des territoires." *note de synthèse sur la gouvernance*. Paris: Centre de documentation de l'Urbanisme.

Huault, I. DiMaggio, P. and Powell, W. 2009. "Des organisations en quête de légitimité." In *Les Grands Auteurs en Management*, edited by S Charreire and I Huault, Paris: EMS, 2nde edition.

Isard, W. 1954. *Localisation an space economy: general theory relating industrial location, market and areas, land use and urban structure*, Cambridge: MIT Press.

Jeffery, N. 2009. *Stakeholder Engagement: A Road Map to Meaningful Engagement*. Cranfield University.

Laffont, J.J. 1998. *Fondements de l'économie publique VI*. Cours de théorie microéconomique, Paris: Economica.

Leborgne, D. Lipietz, A. 1988. "L'après fordisme et son espace." *Les temps modernes* 501.

Leca, B. 2006. "Pas seulement des Lemmings. Les relations entre les organisations et leur environnement dans le néo-institutionnalisme sociologique." *Finance Contrôle Stratégie* 9, 4, (décembre): pp. 67-86.

Lee, C.M. Miller, W. F. Gong Hancock, M. and Rowen, H.S. 2000. *The Silicon Valley Edge*. Stanford: Stanford University Press.

Leloup, F. Moyard, L. and Pecqueur, B. 2005. "La gouvernance territoriale comme nouveau mode de coordination territoriale?" *Géographie Economie et Société* 4, 7: pp. 321-332.

Maby, J. 2008. "Gouvernance et territoire." In *Actes du séminaire Gouvernance des terroirs du vin*. Bordeaux: UMR ADES.

Maillat, D. 1992. "La relation des entreprises innovatrices avec leur milieu." In *Entreprises innovatrices et développement territorial*, edited by D Maillat and J.C Perrin. Paris: GREMI, IRES.

Marshall, A. 1890. *Principles of Economics*. London, Macmillan. 2 Tomes, Gamma 1971.

Meyer, J. and Rowan, B. 1977. "Institutionalized Organizations: Formal Structure as Myth and Ceremony." *American Journal of Sociology* 83: pp. 340-363.

Mitchell, R. K. Agle, B.R. Wood, D.J. 1997. "Toward a theory of stakeholder identification and salience: Defining the principle of who and what really counts." *Academy of Management Review* 22, 4: pp. 853-886.

Mueller, D.C. 1980. Public Choice, Cambridge: University Press.

Mueller D.C. 1989. *Public choice II*. Cambridge: University Press.

Mueller D.C. 1997. *Perspectives on Public Choice. A Handbook*. Cambridge: University Press.

Olander, S. and Landin, A. 2005. "Evaluation of stakeholder influence in the implementation of construction project." *International Journal of Project Management* 23, 4, (May): pp. 321–328.

Parmar, B. L. Freeman, R. E. Harrison, J. S. Wicks, A. C. Purnell, L. and De Colle, S. 2010. "Stakeholder Theory: The State of the Art." *The Academy of Management Annals* 4, 1: pp. 403-445.

Pearsons J. 1952. *The Social System.* London: Routledge.

Perrin, J.C. 1990. "Réseaux, districts, milieux-contribution à une définition économique du territoire." Colloque de l'ASRDLF, *Mondialisation de l'économie et développement des territoires.* Saint-Etienne, 3/4 Sept.

Perrin, J.C. 1992. "Pour une révision de la Science Régionale, une approche par les milieux." *Revue Canadienne des sciences régionales* 15, 2.

Perroux, F. 1950. "*Les espaces économiques.*" In *Économie appliquée Tome III,* edited by ISEA. Paris.

Perroux, F. 1961. *L'économie du XXème siècle.* Paris: P.U.F.

Postema, T. Groen, A. and Krabbendam, K. 2012. "A model to evaluate stakeholder dynamics during innovation implementation." *International Journal of Innovation Management* 16, 5.

Quevit, M. 1991. "Innovative environments and local/international linkages." In *enterprise strategy: a framework for analysis,* edited by R Camagni, London and New York.

Reynaud, J.D. 1988. "Les régulations dans les organisations: régulation de contrôle et régulation autonome." *Revue française de Sociologie* 29: pp. 5-18.

Reynaud, J.D. 1997. *Les règles du jeu. L'action collective et la régulation sociale.* Paris: Armand Collin.

Rowley, T.J. 1997. "Moving Beyond Dyadic Ties: A Network Theory of Stakeholder Influences." *Academy of Management Review* 22, 4: pp. 887-910.

Scott, R. W. 2001. *Institutions and organizations.* Thousand Oaks, CA: Sage, 2nd.

Simon, H. 1957. "A Behavioral Model of Rational Choice". In *Models of Man, Social and Rational: Mathematical Essays on Rational Human Behavior in a Social Setting.* New York: Wiley.

Stoker, G. 1998. "Cinq propositions pour une théorie de la gouvernance." *Revue internationale des Sciences Sociales* 155, Paris: UNESCO.

Thoenig, J.C. 1993. "La sociologie des organisations face au local" In *A la recherche du local,* edited by A Mabileau. Paris: Logiques économiques, L'harmattan.

Tolbert, P.S. and Zucker, L.G. 1996. "The Institutionalization of Institutional Theory." In *Handbook of Organization Studies,* edited by S Clegg, C Hardy and WR Nord, 175-190. London Thousand Oaks New Delhi: Sage Publication.

Vaesken, P. 1996. "L'environnement Territorialisé: Un nouveau concept de structuration de l'environnement dans la stratégie de l'entreprise." *Colloque AIMS,* Mai Lille.

Vaesken, P. 2011. "Régulation et Gouvernance en économie sociale et solidaire. Un modèle pour comprendre l'innovation sociale territoriale." In *Les territoires au cœur du présent et de l'anticipation.* Paris: Céreq.

Vaesken, P. 2014. "Développement durable et régulation: Vers un nouveau paradigme de la gouvernance mondiale." In *L'environnement et le développement durable: Les nouvelles alternatives,* edited by B Nadir, Rabat: Université Mohamed V Souissi.

Vaesken, P. and Zafiropoulou, M. 2008a. "Les parties prenantes dans l'articulation de la régulation et de la gouvernance d'un territoire d'économie sociale et solidaire." *Colloque de l'AGRH,* Dakar Sénégal.

Vaesken, P. and Zafiropoulou, M. 2008b. "Economie Sociale: une pratique de régulation territoriale." *Working paper* 5 CIRIEC.

Vidal De La Blache, 1905, "Tableau de la géographie de la France". *Histoire de France* (1903-1922), edited by E Lavisse en 28 volumes, Tome 1.

Von Thünen, J.H. 1926. *Der isolierte staat.* Hamburg: beziehung auf landwirtschaft und nationalökonomie.

Weber, M. 1919. *Le savant et le politique.* Paris: Plon 1959.

Weick, K. 1969. *The social psychology of organizing.* Addison-Wesley.

Zaoual, H. 2004. "Croyances et gouvernance, vers une théorie de la gouvernance située." In *gouvernance locale au Maghreb,* REMALD, Thèmes Actuels, 46.

Zaoual, H. 2008. *Développement Durable des territoires, économie sociale, environnement et innovations.* Paris: L'Harmattan.

Chapter 2

New Strategical Design for
Territorial Development

2.1 Territorial policy and citizens' acceptance

The main objective of this chapter is to expand the scope of the Territorial Values Framework (TVF) to the issue of citizens' acceptance of territorial offers conveyed by this policy. In this chapter, the key concerns are: In a territorial action plan, how to make territorial offers as attractive as possible to citizens? How to motivate citizens to accept offers that ensure the implementation of the action plan? How to act on citizen's decision-making process to achieve the objectives of the action plan better? How this intention could broaden the understanding of governance and regulation?

These questions, and among them this of influence, are essential for TVF. The crossings between governance / regulation and Bottom-up / Top-down offer strategic and operational means to manage the dynamics of territorial development on the sole condition that citizen's acceptance is at the heart of the process. These questions offer territories the approaches that allow them to regenerate and develop through new or better offers. Through the acceptance and commitment of citizens, it is the question of the dynamics of territorial change on the economic, societal, environmental or cultural level that is raised. Their inclusion should prevent TVF and the planners of the action plan from taking for granted that citizens' behavior conforms to standards or financial incentives. The TVF's approach to acceptance focuses on the motivations of citizens to engage in the process of value creation and the different forms taken by this creation as well as their consequences on the territorial action plan. The TVF has to ensure its realism and operational effectiveness by confronting a specific tension: that of the consequences of the bargaining power of citizens, who are stakeholders of territorial action on the achievement of plan objectives.

This bargaining power of citizens can take various forms. It may be null and void when the territorial action plan is based on laws and regulations where non-compliance is considered an offense rather than presenting a real power to choose proposed offers. From the tax payment collected by the territory to the adoption of eco-responsible heating methods or from the use of medical prevention devices to the use of carpooling, the range of expressions of citizens' bargaining power is wide.

The range expands all roles of stakeholders characterized by Mitchell et al. (1997), presenting that the bargaining power of stakeholders is based on the *power* exercised by these stakeholders, the *urgency* of their request, and the *legitimacy* of this request. The question of citizens' acceptance thus clearly places the TVF in the perspective of territorial development and social innovation. From the managerial point of view, it makes of influence and means to strengthen a necessary condition for the implementation of its objectives.

The introduction of behavioral science and behavioral economics into public policy design is certainly not new (Kahneman 2003). The "Nudge theory" and the "libertarian paternalism" (Thaler and Sunstein 2008), for example, try to influence citizens to make non-coercive decisions that are favorable to the objectives of a plan. They are both an "architecture of choice", from an anti-obesity action (like color code on packaging) to the use of stairs rather than escalators (like musical staircase) preserving the users' cardiovascular system. They bring about debate and criticism.

However, this chapter does not intend to use this approach to influence citizens' choices with consideration of the findings that "cognitive biases" (Kahneman and Tversky 1979) can sometimes "remove them from the right decisions" and for which nudge can help create "societal well-being".

The TVF, without denying the usefulness of "nudges" and without entering into the critical debate, tends to address the problem that influences citizens' decisions from their judgment of satisfaction. Instead of building an "architecture of choice" that exploits conceptual biases derived from the "prospect theory" (Kahneman and Tversky 1979), the TVF aims to offer theoretical and practical approaches that allow territorial action plans to manage in situations where citizens are consciously active, cooperative and collaborative stakeholders. This conceptual framework appears to be the only one available to provide theoretical and practical approaches to development and social innovation in the territory.

The TVF, therefore, has to deliver the tools of influence based on arguments and the conscious mechanisms of persuasion. The remained question is how to make a citizen accept these offers that fit his personal or collective interests? Even if only in his intergenerational interests, the offers affect the common goods or the treatment of the environmental crisis.

The TVF seeks to integrate the citizen as a consumer, a beneficiary, and/or a taxable person, depending on the roles that the territorial action plan gives him. The needs for theoretical and conceptual references allow the TVF to conduct development and social innovation. It proposes offers that can be accepted and sought later on, and thus creates its attractiveness through the dynamic towards achieving the objectives.

2.2 Territorial policy: the servitization underway

The TVF borrows useful concepts derived from the theory of service, which is oriented towards producer/client co-production into the service provision (Prahalad 2004 and Lovelock and Gummesson 2004). This co-production is a combination of resources of a producer and a customer, whether he is a beneficiary free of charge or a client leading to a transformative act that will give him uses. For instance, a citizen agrees to submit a request for obtaining financial assistance from a territorial administration for his home thermal insulation project. The drafting of the file and the contribution of his property combined with financial assistance will transform his home and give rise to a use in terms of energy saving. The theory of resources and their combination in a co-production interface between territorial offer providers and citizens open up a conceptual framework in which the TVF draws its analyses and operational proposals.

The service approach covers the bulk of territorial missions at national, regional and/or local level: from training to social and professional integration, from tourism to transportation, from environmental protection to culture and so forth. It specifies a considerable number of proposals contained in the territorial action plans. It brings them together under a common trait, specific to the service offer: the absence of transferring ownership from the service provider to the client (Lovelock and Gummesson 2004).

The service generates uses that cannot be materialized by the mere delivery to buyers or beneficiaries of particular commodities (Lambin 1990). The concept of service allows the TVF to encompass the diversity of specificities of the territorial offers, such as the provision of common goods or the reduction of consumption (like non-use of the personal car, reduced resource consumption, fight against smoking, etc.), to restrain a demand deemed socially or environmentally undesirable.

The territorial offer, in this theoretical context, is essentially understandable with the idea of combining resources from both territorial service providers and users. It particularly sheds light on the processes of their acceptance. Acceptance does not operationally mean a decision that acquires a good but an entry into the process of resource combination leading to a transformation in which the uses take their value for the user (Moeller 2010). This entry into the combination process requires users to bring resources, which come (Flieβ and Kleinaltenkamp 2004) from users themselves as persons (health, sport, etc.) or their physical objects (waste treatment, energy saving, etc.). These resources may also include their nominal goods (driving license, investment banking, etc.) or rights (lawyers, etc.), or even their psychic skills (intellectual and emotional).

In the resource theory, service provision deploys resources of all entities who, as stakeholders, associate in offer propositions. They are the prerequisites for any combination. These resources are called "operant" when they are used to produce effects by acting on so-called "operand" resources (installations, data from processing devices, physical resources etc.) (Constantin Lusch 1994) and transform them according to the SDL theory (Service Dominant Logic) (Vargo and Lusch 2004). This co-production is the incorporation of resources from citizen to the processes of a territorial provider (registration for a sport or cultural activity, time in leisure, declaration of professional business, examination, provision of material or financial goods, etc.)

Consequently, the acceptance that the territorial policy should obtain from the beneficiary is, above all, an acceptance to co-produce in order to acquire the service provision. This approach, adopted by the TVF, therefore raises the question of the influence of territorial policies by making the concept of a provider-beneficiary co-production interface a key concept.

In the time flow that defines a before-, during- and after- service interface, the TVF can help with understanding and mastering the modalities of the acceptance of territorial offers by citizens. It designs influential territorial policies by accompanying citizens in a "blueprint" where the before-, during- and after- interface requires specific and persuasive actions. The "blueprint" where citizens experience this interface leads the TVF to integrate the major characteristics of the services that the theory refers to in the form of the IHIP approach[1].

2.3 Blueprinting and the IHIP: for influential territorial policies

The IHIP approach identifies four main characteristics. The first one is what has been regularly debated in the specialized literature under the terms of intangibility (Shostack 1977, Gummesson 2007). It essentially denotes the beneficiary's difficulties in mentally representing what the service is, what will happen at the time of the service encounter, and what kinds of results we can expect (Lovelock 1992). Secondly, heterogeneity is related to variable and contingent interventions, because singular, between contact staff and

---

[1] The IHIP approach presents the four key characteristics of service delivery: Intangibility, heterogeneity, inseparability and perishability. These concepts will be defined later (Zeithaml, Parasuraman and Berry 1985).

beneficiaries engaged with their own resources in the co-production interface (Palmer and Cole 1995). Thirdly, inseparability is associated with the interface itself, and the fact that during the service provision, all or part of the production requires the simultaneous presence, remote or not, of all or part of the beneficiary's resources (physical presence of the beneficiary, personal goods, rights or individual data, etc.). So they can be precisely transformed during the service provision (Moeller 2010). Lastly, perishability (Lovelock and Wright 2001, Edvardson. Gusstafson and Roos 2005), emphasizes the fact that the service becomes extinct when the transformation of the beneficiary's resources is over or when these resources are missing or unavailable. The potential capacity to perform a transformation on them perishes, as Hill (1977) clearly stated, the fact that services cannot be held in a stock is not a physical impossibility but a logical impossibility.

Table 2-1: IHIP characteristics of service

Characteristics	Definition	Main issues to policy Makers
Intangibility	Difficulties for beneficiaries to form mental pictures of the service and its effects.	Making the producers' resources available for their offer propositions as tangible as possible. Communicating answers: What am I being offered? How is this going to happen? What can I expect?
Heterogeneity	Difficulties of the service provider and the beneficiary to give the same resources continuously to combine.	Reducing individual differences among service providers. Identifying the resources that the beneficiaries are actually able to engage in the service encounter.
Inseparability	Difficulties to optimize the provider-beneficiary encounter by creating perceived positive experiences and trying to extend the inseparability.	Reduce-simplifying or enriching the service interface depending on its pleasant or unpleasant nature. Knowing the positive externalities of the beneficiaries' uses beyond the service provision once it is over.
Perishability	Difficulties to support and extend the reality of offers when the uses are achieved and to develop loyalty.	Proposing values in use related to the externalities of the intended uses following the service provision. Opening new encounters of value co-creation from positive externalities observed

In this context, the TVF and the territorial action plans are able to gain influence with beneficiaries, if operational measures can reduce the difficulties associated with each of these IHIP characteristics.

Intangibility, thus, appears to be one of the most important and strategic characteristics in the acceptance by the beneficiaries of the service offer. The intangibility of services comes from the difficulties of beneficiaries to perceive a mental representation of the service proposition and to evaluate it before, during and after the service. One may ask questions like "What am I being offered? How is this going to happen? What can I expect?" The difficulty extends to three types of qualities (search, experience, credence) that characterize the service provision (Zeithaml 1981). These qualities are the search for means of the territorial action plans to prevent this risk of loss of influence related to perishability and difficulties to build beneficiary loyalty. Through perishability, the problem of the influence of territorial policies is focused on after-service provision management: how to preserve and extend beyond this provision the value creation regarding supporting the beneficiary loyalty?

2.3.1 Values propositions in territorial policies: creating values to influence

The TVF raises the influential issue from a question: what are citizens able to accept among the value propositions contained in the action plan? To address this issue, the TVF drops the classic transactional perspective of defining value in favor of a collaborative approach: all stakeholders can act together and in varying forms of value creation (Prahalad and Ramaswamy 2004). The notion of value thus takes a subjective and phenomenological perspective in the TVF (Edvardsson, Tronvoll, and Gruber, 2011). The value is analysed here as perceived by the beneficiaries (Gale and Wood 1994, Woodruff 1997).

Value, as a source of influence, implies being observed in all the modes of its creation. They involve service-producing stakeholders and beneficiaries. The TVF identifies these different modes of creation and highlights particularly the ways of mutual value creation in a territorial plan.

These values and their modes of creation should be specified in the TVF. The question is how it can solicit, animate, and develop these modes to make offer proposition as influential as possible. The problems of acceptance and influence are related to the value propositions that will be offered, primarily concerning the values in use. They are the final objectives of territorial service provision that dominate all the TVF. However, to develop practical recommendations, it mainly uses three types of values. These three values are potential values, values in exchange, and values in use[2]. They represent the crucial goals of the action plan to propose.

After presenting these three types of values, the TVF completes its conceptual framework for territorial action by offering its conception of the possible modes of value creation. These modes, as defined above, proceed by the integration of resources and the transformation of all parties of the territorial action plan. Then, it is necessary to question the TVF by defining through governance, regulations, Bottom-up and Top-down chart: what are the possible contributions of the values and their creation modes in the design of the territorial offers and the influential action plans?

Using these three types of values, the designers of the action plan can support the attractiveness and acceptance of the main forms of offers. Three criteria warrant them: 1) the vividness of mental evocation of propositions by the potential values; 2) the facilitation of psychological and physical accesses to co-produce by values in exchange; and 3) the quality of uses and their possible extensions by the values in use. Each of these values plays a dominant and differentiated role at each time phase (before, during, and after) of the service's blueprint. The potential values are mainly related to before-service delivery, the values in exchange appear during the service provision and the values in use are essentially released when the service is rendered. Potential value depends on the ability of all service-producing stakeholders to make their resources attractive for propositions that are likely to be accepted by the beneficiary.

Potential value calls for all improvements or innovations that can evoke as fully as possible. The human, technical and financial relevance of the resources are thus gathered. When service producers help beneficiaries to form an accurate mental picture of how the service provision will take place and what the benefits to be expected, they also produce potential values (table 2-2).

Value in exchange (table 2-3) is expressed in the co-production interface when the resources of both parties are combined. Value in exchange aims at developing the service interface to promote the availability and accessibility of resources for their transformation to its expected uses (Moeller 2008). Thanks to the technology of digitalized interface, it is, for example, to reinforce the user-friendliness of the procedures that combine the resources, to help the co-production or even simply to treat the possible dysfunctions related to the transaction, and to reduce the unpleasantness of some of these situations

---

[2] The three stages of the service provision -FTU framework -(Facilities, Transformation, Usage)- see Moeller, S, (2008), Customer Integration – A key to an Implementation Perspective of Service Provision, Journal of Service Research,11, 2, 197-210, and the blueprinting are strongly underpinned this presentation of values.

(Rush hour, waiting time, behavior of other beneficiaries, etc.) (Griffiths and Gilly 2012). Value in exchange also refers to the beneficiary and his service experience individually or collectively (Berry and Seiders 2008, Tombs and Mc Coll-Kennedy 2010). For example, it is to provide solutions to better support the heterogeneity of the resources provision, the second property of the service (Moeller 2008), such as courses for kids or visually impaired people in a museum, walk-in services, etc. It acts directly on the values in exchange proposed by the service provider. Value in exchange is then a part of social practices or social bonds born from service experiences in relation to interface staff or other consumers. The establishment of social links around a collective project or proximity or the organization of solidarity to carry out a shared project can also create value in exchange.

Table 2-2: Blueprint phases and potential value

	Phase 1 Blueprint	*Phase 2 Blueprint*	*Phase 3 Blueprint*	*Phase 4 Blueprint*
Blueprint Phases	*Get beneficiaries to accept the offer and recruit beneficiaries*	*Take into account the conditions of the combination of resources and their transformation*	*Deliver uses, observe and take advantage of their unforeseen positive effects*	*Retain beneficiaries and co-create with them new values*
Potential Value (Essentially before service provision) *Clearly visualize and gain a concrete idea of the offer proposition and its effects.*	Strategic choice of ways to communicate about "everything we can do to you"	Strategic choice of help to customers to represent themselves accurately the course of co-production	Strategic communication on examples of effects or benefits derived from intended uses and devices for collecting and tracking unplanned uses.	Strategic proposition of new values in use, related to positive externalities of intended uses, and derived from monitoring devices

The value in use (table 2-4) is primarily attached to the after-service provision. It is fully appreciated when the delivery is accomplished and the beneficiary's resources are no longer integrated into the combination and transformation processes at work during the service interface. Value in use can, therefore, be defined as "the propensity of the use or consumption of a product or service to increase perceived well-being" (Grönroos 2008). In the theory of keeping with customer integration and the concepts of combining and transforming ones' resources, the TVF asserts that the creation of value in use can occur during the interface. It is particularly the case when the transformation of the beneficiary's resources is accompanied by consumer experience, sources of well-being and sought for itself, such as a beauty treatment session or a spa.

Table 2-3: Blueprint phases and value in exchange

	Phase 1 Blueprint	*Phase 2 Blueprint*	*Phase 3 Blueprint*	*Phase 4 Blueprint*
Blueprint Phases	*Get beneficiaries to accept the offer and recruit beneficiaries*	*Take into account the conditions of the combination of resources and their transformation*	*Deliver uses, Observe and take advantage of their unforeseen positive effects*	*Retain beneficiaries and co-create with them new values*
Value in exchange (essentially during and after service Provision)	Strategic choice of instructions to communicate to stakeholders and beneficiaries the easiest way to combine and transform resources to get the intended uses	Strategic creation of a service encounter that promotes co-production from provider-beneficiary resources. Make encounters sources of the most satisfying production of value in exchange and experiential value for the beneficiaries	Enhance strategically beneficiaries' ability to develop positive externalities (non-intended values) after they have left the sphere of service provision. Maintain means of contacts and exchanges (platform...)	Promote all the new values in exchanges as positive externalities of intended uses. Develop new encounters to take them into account and prepare new values co-creation

Attention should be paid to diagnose interface situations that can be unappreciated. These situations are often that a beneficiary essentially brings his physical resources (transport, body care, etc.) at the time of transforming a consumption experience whose "unpleasant" character becomes a sensitive point of service. In cases where the transformation is deemed unpleasant and the consumption experience has no value in use, the service must include post-provision benefits that outweigh the sacrifices during the transformation period (Radford and Sridhar 2005).

One of the peculiarities of the value in use is that beneficiaries can benefit from the value in use without the direct use of the offer. In a social and territorial context, value in use can come from indirect interactions related to the influence of the users themselves on those ones around them. It can result in the propagation of meanings, symbols, practices or recommendations

(Buchanan and Dawson 2007, Vallaster and Von Wallpach 2013). It also makes value "in use" a so-called value "in context" (Vargo 2008).

Table 2-4: Blueprint phases and value in use

	Phase 1 Blueprint	*Phase 2 Blueprint*	*Phase 3 Blueprint*	*Phase 4 Blueprint*
Blueprint Phases	*Get beneficiaries to accept the offer and recruit beneficiaries*	*Take into account the conditions of the combination of resources and their transformation*	*Deliver uses, Observe and take advantage of their unforeseen positive effects*	*Retain beneficiaries and co-create with them new values*
Value in use (essentially after service provision) *Deliver all the intended values in use promised in the offer proposition. Secure beneficiaries' loyalty by co-creating new values for policy development*	Strategic communication to give beneficiaries the most vivid representation of the intended values in use contained in the offer proposition and show the policy's interest to develop new ones with beneficiaries	If the conditions of the resources combination and their transformation by producers-beneficiaries are very different from one another propose to take these differences into account to deliver specific values and values in use according to the specific conditions of the service provision	Show that the territorial policy plans to observe all the unforeseen positive effects of the intended uses. These externalities can be collected and new encounters will be processed to exploit and generalize these values in use as well as possible.	Open new encounters to co-create new values in use from these externalities and develop new offer propositions where beneficiaries are prime resources integrators

In short, the TVF gives more consideration to the last form of value which integrates potential value, value in exchange or in use and value in context.

It is known as experiential value (Holbrook 2006). This value, as all those presented before, is always created by beneficiaries. It draws for its creation in the direct or indirect interactions between the stakeholders of the service offered. It adds to the set of values the hedonic dimension of the value. The experiential value raises a key questioning of territorial policies: that of the values sought as a means of pursuing a personal objective (extrinsic value) or an end in itself (intrinsic value) such as, for example, the common goods. The experiential value allows us to comprehend the motivations of the beneficiaries and to integrate them, as many sensitive points, in the completion of the territorial action plans. This consideration can be further refined and essentially allows the action plan to better develop the contents of potential values and in exchange. Finally, two other dimensions should be added to the experiential value: the value can refer to a personal benefit (self-orientation) and other benefits (others-oriented). Thus, one can explore, for example, the offers of leisure or well-being as intrinsic and self-oriented; childcare facilities or dependence assistance as extrinsic and self-oriented; and environmental issues as intrinsic, and others-oriented or socio-cultural activities as extrinsic and others-oriented.

2.3.2 The levers of influence of the territorial plan: the modes of value creation.

With the IHIP characteristics and the blueprint, as sensitive points of an influential conception of the offer proposition, the conceptual framework extends to all these values and to their implementation, as key indicators of the persuasive power of the territorial action plan.

In this context, the TVF seeks to apply. To refine the strategic approach in which the TVF tries to achieve its objectives, the framework needs to be enriched. An analysis of the different ways of creating values is required. In addition to the sensitive points of the persuasive action of the plan, it is a question if the dynamic of value creation leads to the acceptance of the beneficiaries and their satisfaction.

The TVF also seeks to understand the modes of value creation that can affect all the stakeholders of the territorial offer in different configurations. It argues that these configurations should allow a preliminary strategic diagnosis to optimize the influence effects of the plan.

The TVF highlights five different modes of value creation. Each of them, beyond the blueprint and the IHIP, offers an experience of different values for beneficiaries according to the dynamics of their creation process. The TVF approach leads to differentiated modes of value creation under a variety of resource combinations that end up with a transformation that delivers uses.

The nature of combinations and transformations leads to collaborative modes that offer stakeholders and beneficiaries shares and jointly create value. Thus, to select modes of value creation, the TVF accepts the principle of the degree of collaboration or cooperation among all the offer stakeholders and the beneficiaries to produce an optimal amount of value in exchange for an optimal amount of value in use or in context. One of the strategic questions posed to the policymakers comes to: How does each offer of the plan imply a relatively complex form of engagement, exchange, interaction, learning, and reciprocity for optimal production of values? For responding to this question, the dynamics of the influence of the plan are tested. According to the answer, the practical and financial commitments of the plan differ.

Based on such a question, the TVF proposes five significant ways of value creation. The first way is the least collaborative where the producers of the territorial offer are essentially the designers of the value propositions, and the beneficiaries then become the "facilitators" (Cova and Dalli 2009) of the delivery of uses in this situation. The second way can take the form of a co-production of values in a context of resources combination where the designers of the territorial offer are considered "prime resources integrators", as demonstrated in the subsections below. The last ways refer to the richest value creation in terms of collaboration or cooperation qualified as citizens' initiatives in the territorial plans: those of value co-creation without overlooking possible forms of capturing and transferring values, or even co-destruction of value. Each of these ways has to be defined.

Predesigned Value

At the first level of complexity of the resources combination, the value can simply come from a predesigned creation process. In this case, the creation of value itself depends primarily on the objective pursued by the producer and is seen as a means of exerting influence through a well-controlled response to the known expectations of a beneficiary. This one is then a simple "facilitator" of the delivery of the values in use. His consent involves a few personal resources, because it essentially affects the goods intended in the action plan to a simple transfer of property (Christmas gifts from a municipality to the elders, regular sales and exchanges for clothing, the distribution of school awards, etc.). This mode of value creation appears in the action plan as purely transactional. It reduces the production of value to a general theoretical principle that certain streams of research have nevertheless described as co-creation by nature (Vargo and Lusch 2008).

The position of TVF is to assert that imposing such a theoretical generality and retaining the general and undifferentiated principle of co-creation by nature have practical consequences. Such a principle makes the concrete examination of the means of influence and the strategies of territorial offers particularly difficult. The search for influence concretely requires a more precise definition of stakeholders' and beneficiaries' places and roles in the value creation.

The TVF, following the research on the "encounter design" (Payne, Storbacka and Frow 2008) and the management of the value co-creation processes does not adopt the overall theory of the co-creation by nature in order to better apprehend the mechanisms of influence that can inspire the value propositions of public policies.

Co-production

The co-production of values between the offer stakeholders and the beneficiaries defines the second level of complexity in the resources combination. The co-production of value provides a concrete basis for better developing the influence of territorial suppliers. As described above, co-production involves an interface, even a reduced or remote one, between the providers of the offer and the beneficiaries. This interface, as a contact point, can be made attractive by the service providers from elements like advertising, public relations, open days, etc., which propose potential values to the beneficiaries. Besides, the interface supposes a resource combination in view of a transformation. During the service provision, this union can also be a source of values in exchange that service providers develop to be influential.

In this sense, the co-production of value is limited to a direct collaboration between actors during the service encounter. It involves the participation of stakeholders (citizens, public organizations, firms, etc.) in carrying out the activities of combination and transformation of resources in values in use. Consumers in this situation are the co-producers of their own offer (Witell, Kristensson, Gustafsson and Löfgren 2011).

The co-production takes an important place in the operational presentation of the TVF. Regarding the attractiveness of the service provision to beneficiaries, the co-production should strategically target the usual values that combine the motivation of the beneficiary with the engagement in the combination of resources as potential values. It is to find all facilities to co-produce as values in exchange and finally to produce the greatest number of desired benefits as values in use. For instance, after watching Disney TV commercial parents bring children who show their enthusiasm for an announcement of a visit to Disneyland.

It is possible to extend the strategic scope of value co-production to include these two other forms of value co-production: co-innovation and open innovation (Enkel, Gassmann and Chesbrough 2009).

Co-innovation and open innovation

These two modes of value creation are based on the idea of resource exchange where stakeholders are both providers and beneficiaries (Payne et al. 2008). They develop new resources in innovation-oriented processes. These processes are characterized by inbound and outbound knowledge flows (Chesbrough 2006, Huizingh 2011). They are likely to create innovation through shared organizational value (Lee et al. 2012). These two modes often rely on online platforms where actors can interact and exchange. They differ by the fact that, unlike open innovation, co-innovation refers to a process in which the involved actors are selected as a priori (Roser, De Fillippi and Samson 2013). In open innovation, co-produced offers are developed and can be consumed by other individuals.

Value co-creation

Value co-creation is the last vital dimension of value creation. The TVF retains the following premise of value co-creation: value co-creation is a joint initiative where service providers and beneficiaries exchange resources and create value together (Prahalad and Ramaswamy 2004). In the first place, co-creation differs from co-production by generating value for all the involved producers and beneficiaries. Another difference, while co-production is limited to collaboration during the service provision, co-creation also shows interactions during the consumption of offers when the values in use are issued. In the second place, the concept of value co-creation is based on the idea that beneficiaries can benefit from value without the direct use of the offer. It implies that, in co-creation, the values in use can also be values in context resulting from indirect interactions, influences, and parallel practices, as illustrated before. Value co-creation poses public policy and the strategic issues of maximizing values in use, experiential values, and values in context for beneficiaries (Merz, Yi and Vargo 2009).

This objective leads to integrating the service providers into the consumption processes and enriching the intended uses. This is a possible result of the strategy of monitoring the initiatives of the beneficiaries during their consumption and the implementation of new encounters in order to prolong those already conceived.

As mentioned above, value co-creation in the territorial values framework is not by nature. It is conditioned to a strategy of the service providers who observe the initiatives of beneficiaries concerning unexpected uses. It proposes new resources to combine during new encounters so that the uses resulting from the inventiveness of beneficiaries can serve as a basis and a relay for new co-created proposals. The TVF draws from this conception of value co-creation this strategic consequence: territorial policies must be able, whatever the "perishability" of the offer, to implement means of collecting data and setting up new platforms. They should contribute to harnessing inclusive and collaborative processes based on positive externalities conceived as the effects of citizen consumption and their intended uses.

Positive externalities are unforeseen positive effects of the uses delivered by the service provision. They concretize the whole interest of value co-creation to reinforce the attractiveness of territorial offers through the intensity of interactive extensions between stakeholders. For example, a municipality has offered an introduction of auto mechanics to teenagers from disadvantaged neighborhoods. When the teenagers can apprehend that disassembled mechanical parts are unexpectedly used to create assemblies in a playful way, the municipality is likely to think of relaunching an offer of an artistic workshop to make mobile sculptures and gathering them in an exhibition. The TVF will speak of co-creation of values mobilizing all the concepts presented above.

In essence, value co-creation touches on three types of values: potential, in exchange, and in use. It invites a broader conception of value creation resulting from direct or indirect interactions between actors, and then acts as positive externalities producing unexpectedly but exploitable new values including experiential values or in context, which can be employed by territorial strategy.

Designing and anticipating the interactional supports that make this co-creation possible is hence one of the central issues of territorial policies. Co-creation is a carrier of citizen initiatives, enrichment of social capital and/or the psychological and physical well-being of citizens. Its implementation should reinforce the influence of the action plans and contribute to the achievement of their objectives. Co-creation is also an opportunity for the stakeholders of the territorial offer to enrich their operational approaches of the actors that are beyond the roles of the stakeholders defined in chapter 4 (Mitchel, Agle and Wood 1997).

To outline the territorial diagnosis and to design an attractive action plan through its mastery of value creation, two significant notions should be discussed in details: the transfer or capture of value and the destruction of value.

The transfer or capture of value consists in integrating uses that are not delivered by territorial actions with the uses proposed by the action plan. It can be exemplary or innovative uses, civic witnesses, economic, social, cultural or environmental issues that illustrate the intentions of the action plan, and serving as references that the action plan would like to generalize. Labels can be essential tools for the transfer and capture of value. They can express the support of policymakers for value creation from the citizen initiatives.

The label is implemented by policymakers from a set of specifications on a theme and distinctive characters that elect an action and its usages as a specific goal. It can thus play the role of intermediation tool among the partners of the territory, by encouraging their collaboration. The transfer or capture may also take the form of a simple reference to uses to which the territorial action plan declares to associate or to receive the guarantee.

The destruction of value, as a negative externality of the territorial action, should be the object of all policymakers' attention. It appears as the opposite of value co-creation. It can lead to a decrease in value for at least one of the stakeholders or beneficiaries of the plan (Plé and Chumpitaz Cacères 2010). This destruction results from inappropriate or unexpected uses of resources from the viewpoint of the service producers. Abuse may be accidental or intentional. It can be relational (such as under or over-participation), interpersonal (such as verbal or physical abuse), or related to goods (such as property abuse or fraud). This destruction may occur after the delivery of the uses or during the co-production and the combination of the resources to be transformed. In this sense, the value co-destruction can essentially affect the values in exchange or in use of the service proposition, which eventually influences the experiential values. It should sensitize policymakers on the state of the commitment of all stakeholders and beneficiaries and only pledge to master the intrinsic perishability of the territorial offer by maintaining motivation and loyalty (Simon 1991).

Table 2-5: The five modes of Value Creation

Mode of Value Creation	Main characteristics
Predesigned Value	It is the least collaborative value creation. The predesigned value is mainly created by the producers of the offer. In this way of creating value, the beneficiary is only a "facilitator" of the value delivered. It is purely transactional. The beneficiary's resources are few requested in the definition and implementation of the value
Value co-production	It is a way of creating value that involves an active interface. In this encounter, producer and beneficiary combine their resources. Without this resources integration and direct collaboration in the service provision, no value creation is possible.
Co-innovation	Co-innovation describes a process during which the actors involved are selected a priori. Internal and external information flows converge to create organizational value directed towards innovation.
Open innovation	Open innovation is a process without actors' selection. Internal or external information flows can be used by everyone in the design and in the implementation or consumption of the innovation
Value co-creation	Co-creation is a joint initiative whereby providers and beneficiaries attempt to create value together. The co-creation of value in TVF involves interactions allowing the exploitation of positive externalities that are added to the values promised by the offer to produce new values for both providers and beneficiaries

All the active concepts in the analysis of influence and acceptance means of territorial offers are thus proposed. It is now plausible to examine how these concepts can help to optimize this influence and acceptance by integrating them into the TVF and the two key dimensions of its functioning: regulation and governance.

2.4 Regulation and Governance of territorial policies: how to optimize the attractiveness and acceptability of territorial offers?

The first chapter introduces definitions of governance and regulation. The current chapter seeks an answer or answers to the questions: what are their places and roles in the implementation of territorial offers to make them attractive and promote their acceptance among beneficiaries? How does regulation or governance intervene in the sensitive matters of the territorial offer, such as intangibility, heterogeneity, inseparability and perishability, and obstacles to its acceptance and the satisfaction and loyalty of citizens? How do they contribute to the selection and animation of the ways of value creation as levers with which the offer proposition takes its power of influence?

The TVF has shown that governance and regulation are constantly interaction to analyze, predict and animate territorial actions. Territorial offers are thus designed on the principle of mobilizing all stakeholders including beneficiaries and optimizing all the combinations that can create values for all the actors as a collective actor. The driving value of the governance-regulatory interaction comes from its ability to define specific modes of territorial interventions based on the facilitation to create value and to innovate in this creation.

2.4.1 Regulation

Here, regulation takes a specific meaning beyond the analysis of the first chapter. In the TVF, regulation is the offer-centered and operational part of the interaction in territorial interventions. It is thus essential as the starting point and the foundation of the interaction to be put in place in the approach of the territorial action plan. It consists of:

- Selecting the forms of value creation to be put in play and to promote in the territorial plan,

- Defining offer propositions, their concrete contents and their modes of provision delivering promised uses;

- Stimulating various forms of value creation selected by the territorial action plan with appropriate stimuli and ensuring their coherence and their most attractive expression(s);

- Making sure that the offer proposition delivers all the possible forms of value that make this proposition attractive and lead to its ultimate acceptance. Through innovation and enrichment, it elicits new values using new forms to create them.

The indispensable tasks of defining regulation are thus the design of the value creation scenarios that present in all the offer propositions according to the contexts of weak or strong institutionalization, the choice of the concrete contents of the offer propositions, and the search for the stimuli to make the proposition as attractive as possible to bring about its acceptance.

The regulation also mentions the settings of information collection systems that can take the stock of the values delivered and their level of attractiveness. It prepares new offers by reinventing the places and roles in this value creation of all stakeholders, including beneficiaries.

The regulation operates on a continuum where the tasks described above take place in an organizational framework reduced to emerging initiatives or strongly institutionalized. The regulation thus considers all the concrete means of designing and implementing the offer proposition. It does this by both synchronically opening the accurate details of this proposition and its implementation in a specific context, and diachronically watching over the possible evolutions of such a proposition for its values improvement or enrichment. The regulation then consists of innovating content on a prospective basis or designing how to redistribute the places and roles of the stakeholders in the modes of value creation.

In the same way, the definition of governance presented in the first chapter takes a complementary and operational meaning integrating the developments of this chapter.

2.4.2 Governance

Governance in the TVF focuses on decision-makers or beneficiaries and on the relationships they maintain strategically so that the offer propositions of the plan exist and deliver the expected values. In the same way, the governance supports the new reconfigurations of these relations of actors to find a continuation of the territorial development in other offer propositions. It consists of:

- Finding the best and promising arrangement of the stakeholders in order to optimize the combination of their resources producing the territorial offer;
- Choosing among the actors who will take the places and the roles of the "prime resources integrator" and taking, as such, the initiatives to

gather the producers' resources of the offer and to ensure the conditions of their integration with those of beneficiaries to transform them into values;

- Defining the evolutions, after analysis of the contexts in which the territorial offers are formulated, that these arrangements of stakeholders including the beneficiaries can be taken according to their individual and emerging or institutionalized character;

- Ensuring, in a prospective way, which actors can alternatively take the roles of "prime resources integrator" to activate the dynamics and extend of the action areas of the territorial plan.

The essential functions that define governance are thus the search for collaborations, cooperation and partnerships among producers of the territorial offer in order to gather all the resources that optimize the offer propositions. It does this by both synchronically designating among these actors, "prime resources integrators", which enables the integration of their resources with those of the beneficiaries, and diachronically differentiating the adapted devices of the resource combination after analyzing the contextual elements of the offer proposition on a continuum ranging from the emerging individuals to the strongly institutionalized organizations. Governance then consists of ruling the strategic foresight of territorial actions by favoring at the organizational level the alternating role of "prime resources integrators" for service producers and beneficiaries. Governance gives the action plans as most extensive collaborative framework as possible between stakeholders including beneficiaries, and a dynamic where value propositions bring out others.

All the active dimensions in the design of the territorial action plan now have been presented. These dimensions should help the action plan stakeholders to make a precise decision on what to act in different situations. Additionally, they can help to guide these actions to optimize the effects on the beneficiaries and all the actors in territory. The territorial action plan taking the TVF into account and all its dimensions can blend objectives to sustain individuals or emerging initiatives being rich in potentialities with objectives based on all the resources of the national, regional and local institutions in the territory. The TVF must offer all the means to make the coexistence of this variety of objectives guarantor of the territorial dynamics.

Chapters 3, 4 and 5 finalize the complete vision by proposing three tools that best concretize the main potential questions to ensure that territorial management is truly inspired by the TVF. These three tools in Chapter 3, 4 and 5 present the detailed overview of the Territorial Value Framework, the management of the stakeholders, the quality diagnosis of the territorial offers and the search for territorial innovation, and the practical application of the TVF.

Bibliography

Berry, L.L. and Seiders, K. 2008. "Serving unfair customers." *Business Horizons* 51, 1: pp. 29-37.

Buchanan, D. and Dawson P. 2007. "Discourse and audience: Organizational change as multi-story process." *Journal of Management Studies* 44, 5: pp. 669-686.

Chesbrough, H.W. 2006. *Open Innovation: The new imperative for creating and profiting from technology.* Cambridge, MA: Harvard Business School press.

Constantin, J.A. and Lusch, R. F. 1994. *Understanding Resource Management: How to Deploy Your People, Products and Processes for Maximum Productivity.* Burr Ridge, IL: Irwin.

Cova, B. and Dalli, D. 2009. "Working Consumers: the next step in marketing Theory." *Marketing Theory*, 9, 3: pp. 315-339.

Edvardsson, B. Gustafsson, A. and Roos, I. 2005. "Service portraits in service research: a critical review." *International journal of service industry management* 16, 1: pp. 107-121.

Edvardsson, B. Tronvoll, B. and Gruber, T. 2011. "Expanding understanding of service exchange and value co-creation: a social construction approach." *Journal of the Academy of Marketing Science* 39, 2: pp. 327-339.

Enkel, E. Gassmann, 0. and Chesbrough, H. 2009. "Open R&D and open innovation: exploring the phenomenon." *R&D Management* 39, 4: pp. 311-316.

Flieβ, S. and Kleinaltenkamp, M. 2004. "Blueprinting the service company. Managing service processes efficiently." *Journal of Business Research* 57, 4: pp. 392-404.

Gale, B. and Wood, R.C. 1994. *Managing Customer value: Creating quality and service that customers can see.* New-York, Simon & Schuster.

Griffiths, M.A. and Gilly, M.C. 2012. "Dibs! Customer territorial behaviors." *Journal of Service Research* 15, 2: pp. 131-149.

Grönroos, C. 2008. "Service Logic revisited: who creates value and who co-creates?" *European Business Review* 20, 4: pp. 298-314.

Gummesson. E. 2007. "Exit services marketing- enter service marketing." *Journal of Customer Behaviour* 6, 2: pp. 113-141.

Holbrook, M.B. 2006. "Consumption experience, customer value and subjective personal introspection: an illustrative photographic essay." *Journal of Business Research*, 59, 6: pp. 714-725.

Huizingh, E.K. 2011. "Open innovation: state of the art and future perspectives." *Technovation* 31, 1: pp. 2-9.

Kahneman, D. 2003. "A perspective on judgment and choice: Mapping bounded rationality." *American Psychologist* 58, 9: pp. 697-720.

Kahneman, D. and Tversky, A. 1979. "Prospect Theory: An Analysis of Decision under Risk" *Econometrica* 47, 2 (March): pp. 263-291.

Lambin, J.J. 1990. *Le marketing stratégique: du marketing à l'orientation-marché* 4ième édition. Paris: Ediscience international.

Lee, S.M. Olson, D.L. and Trimi, S. 2012. "Co-innovation: convergenomics, collaboration and co-creation for organizational values." *Management decision* 50, 5: pp. 817-831.

Lovelock, C. and Gummesson, E. 2004. "Wither Service Marketing? In Search of a new Paradigm and Fresh Perspective." *Journal of Service Research* 7, (August): pp. 20-41.

Merz, M.A. Yi, H. and Vargo, S.L, 2009. "The evolving brand logic: a service dominant logic perspective." *Journal of the Academy of Marketing Science* 37, 3: pp. 328-344.

Mitchel, R. Agle, K. and Wood, D. J. 1997. "Toward a Theory of Stakeholder Identification and Salience: Defining the Principle of Who and What Really Counts." *The Academy of Management Review* 22, 4. (Oct.): pp. 853-886.

Moeller, S. 2010. "Characteristics of services –a new approach uncovers their value." *Journal of Services Marketing* 24, 5: pp. 359-368.

Payne, A.F. Storbacka, K. and Frow, P. 2008. "Managing the co-creation of value." *Journal of the Academy of Marketing Science* 36: pp. 83-96.

Plé, L. and Chumpitaz Cacères, R. 2010. "Not always co-creation: introducing interactional co-destruction of value in service service-dominant logic." *Journal of Services Marketing* 24, 6: pp. 430-437.

Prahalad, C. K. 2004. "The Co-creation of Value." *Journal of Marketing* 68, (January), 23: pp. 56-67.

Prahalad, C.K. and Ramaswamy, V. 2004. "Co-creation experiences: the next practice in value creation." *Journal of Interactive Marketing* 18, 3: pp. 5-14.

Radford, S. and Sridhar, S. 2005. "All Co-Production is not Created Equal: A Value Congruence Approach Examining the Degree of Co-Production" AMA educators' Proceedings: Enhancing Knowledge Development in Marketing *American Medical Association*, Chicago: pp. 244-251.

Roser, T. De Fillippi, R. and Samson, A. 2013. "Managing your co-creation mix: co-creation ventures in distinctive contexts." *European Business Review* 25, 1: pp. 20-41.

Simon, H. A. 1991. "Organizations and markets." *the journal of Economic perspectives* 5: pp. 25-44.

Thaler, R. and Sunstein, C. 2008. *Nudge: Improving Decisions about Health, Wealth, and Happiness,* Yale University Press (April) 192.

Tombs, A. and Mc Coll-Kennedy, J.R. 2010. "Social and Spatial influence of customers on other customers in the social service scape." *Autralasian Marketing Journal*, 18, 3: pp. 120-131.

Vallaster, C. and Von Wallpach, S. 2013. "An online discursive inquiry into social dynamics of multi-stakeholder brand meaning co-creation." *Journal of Business Research* 66, 9: pp. 1505-1515.

Vargo, S.L. 2008. "Customer integration and value creation: paradigmatic traps and perspectives." *Journal of Service Research* 11, 2: pp. 211-215.

Vargo, S.L. and Lusch, R.F. 2004. "Evolving a New Service Dominant Logic for Marketing." *Journal of Marketing* 68 (January): pp. 1-17.

Vargo, S.L. and Lusch, R.F. 2008. "Service Dominant Logic: continuing the evolution." *Journal of the Academy of Marketing Science* 36: pp. 1-10.

Witell, L. Kristensson, P. Gustafsson, A. and Löfgren, M. 2011. "Idea generation: customer co-creation versus traditional market research techniques." *Journal of services management* 22, 2: pp. 140-159.

Woodruff, R.B. 1997. "Customer value: the next source for competitive advantage." *Journal of the Academy of Marketing Science* 25, 2: pp. 139-153.

Zeithalm, L.V. 1981, "How Consumer Evaluation Processes Differ between Goods and Services" In *Services Marketing*, edited by C.H Lovelock, Englewoods Cliffs, New York: Prentice Hall.

Zeitham, L.l V.A. Parasuraman, A. and Berry L.L. 1985. "Problems and strategies in service marketing." *Journal of Marketing* 49, 2: pp. 33-46.

Chapter 3

Method and Tool 1: The Territorial Value Framework (TVF)

3.1 Tool 1: The TVF and its operational presentation

The TVF (Territorial Value Framework) offers analyses and development tools for the territories. It appears as the synthesis of tools capable of integrating the approaches by stakeholders and the Cube Service Values (CSV) presented later in Chapters 4 and 5.

These tools should enable to build territorial development strategies based on diagnostic analyses and the implementation of action plans. In this part, to understand the foundations for constructing the TVF, the classic approaches of a territorial diagnosis focusing on territorial development are presented, such as those relating to Top-down versus Bottom-up development (see Section 3.1.1). Using this approach, the TVF seeks to consider the specificities of local development in a managerial vision that is built on the principles of regulation and governance (see Section 3.1.2). Finally, this dual consideration allows access through the TVF to the different types of territorial development available to policymakers (see Section 3.1.3), to understand the situation of their territory and choose an option for its development.

3.1.1 Top-Down versus Bottom-Up development

To improve the functioning of a territory continuously, a territorial policy is required to regulate:

- By offering some propositions that define the content of the services available to the territory;

- By making interaction among these propositions which are brought by public decision-makers and resulting from local initiatives (supported by the various stakeholders of the territory or external to the territory but who interact on it).

Mariam (1997, 2007) defines Top-Down and Bottom-Up as dialectical relationships. These two approaches have to be viewed as complementary and capable of restoring all of the dynamics at work in territorial functioning. At a specific moment in territorial action, their relations can contrast with purely legislative and centralized approaches, based on the principle of "command and control regulation" or what has been referred to as an emerging conception "incentive or performance-based regulation".

The first form of regulation is founded on the exercise of laws or rules whose content is intended to impose or aspire to a general application. The second form refers more to the progressive and, sometimes, contingent implementation of emerging offer propositions. The combination of these two approaches integrates a so-called legislative with cultural or spontaneous vision. It has to find its balance in a regulatory system capable of making a legislative vision coexist, weighted in varying degrees, with a cultural vision.

In this dialectic, everything happens as if the regulation were only a system of back and forth between the legislative and the initiative. However, this vision remains unsatisfactory because it takes into account only the Bottom-up or Top-down approach without proposing the processes in which the various propositions find their stable form and become acceptable. Stabilization thus seeks a balance between the ascendant and the descendant that finalizes the content of the offer while acceptability aims to create a consensus on its attractiveness.

Hargreaves, Haxeltime, Longhurst and Seyfang (2011) provide an initial response by completing the Bottom-Up/Top-Down approach with the Multi-Level Perspective (henceforth, MLP)/Social Practice Theory (henceforth, SPT) vision. The MLP vision accounts for both ascendant (Bottom-up) and descendant (Top-down) approach. In addition, the SPT focuses on the actors' practices and their contribution to the success of the offers by institutionally setting the standards or techniques that should be followed. The point of conciliation between the MLP and the SPT is linked to a negotiation in terms of stabilization and acceptability.

In fact, the MLP/SPT is a non-linear process that integrates three levels of territorial analysis. The first level is an emerging level, which can be the niche of innovations; the second one is a technical regime, which seeks to stabilize the places and roles of the actors and to guarantee the attractiveness and complementarity of the offer propositions; the third one is a legislative level, which defines the hierarchical or authoritarian environment that respects the common interests.

This vision incorporates a dynamic into the classic Bottom-Up/Top-Down vision. It takes into account the levels of legal institutionalization (authoritarian environment), cultural (emerging level), and normative (technical regime).

The following diagram demonstrates this dynamic and interactive approach:

Figure 3-1: The decision-making process in the MLP / SPT

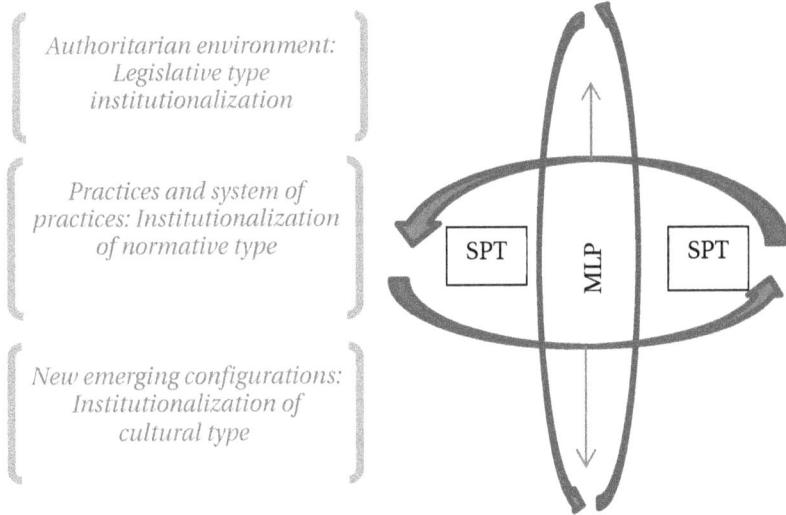

This figure highlights three key elements involved in the decision-making process and involved in the territorial action plan:

- ✓ The SPT appears to be the necessary search for finalization and acceptability (through the development of rules and technical reference systems) of the offer propositions from the Bottom-Up and Top-Down processes carried by the MLP.

- ✓ The MLP/SPT intersection is as an essential moment of negotiation between the "command and control" or the "incentive or performance-based" regulatory processes and the practices of the actors concerned.

- ✓ The crossover (MLP/SPT) highlights the need for analysts and decision-makers to ensure the ability of SPT, as a technical regime, to finalize the offer propositions and to promote their acceptability and attractiveness.

3.1.2 The TVF: a dynamic global system based on the MLP/SPT crossover

This new paradigmatic approach to territorial policies also questions the place and role of the actors in this system. The Vaesken and Zafiropoulou's graph (2008a and 2008b, Vaesken 2012) tries to design an analytical grid that crosses the Top-down/Bottom-up and MLP/SPT approaches with the governance and regulation issues. This grid sheds light upon the place and role of stakeholders in territorial policies. The following diagram demonstrates this dynamic and interactive approach:

Figure 3-2: Crossover between governance and regulation with MLP / SPT

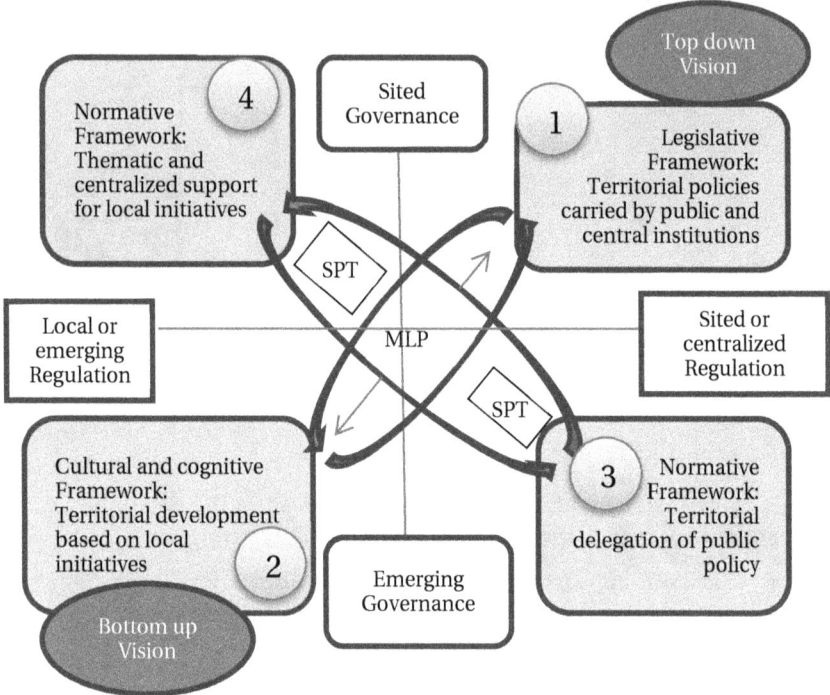

This analytical grid organizes this dynamic and universal system using the opposite forms taken both by regulation and by governance. The first form opposes regulation, from an emerging regulation (right of the horizontal axis) of cultural type to a sited regulation (left of the horizontal axis), of a structured and integrated type, inspired by institutionalization models of legislative or normative type in a territorial context.

The second form opposes an emerging governance (bottom of the vertical axis) of the spontaneous type based on contingent and local initiatives of individuals or groups of individuals to site governance (top of the vertical axis) of the institutional type, having the capacity to define general rules, within the framework of the collective territorial interest.

Figure 3.2 provides an important part of the requisite references for the implementation of the TVF. The TVF proposes to understand the essential features of existing or future territorial policies. The regulation is at the heart of these references that shape territorial policies. It designates the concrete and technical implementation of the guidelines defined by governance at the central or local level. The regulation thus carries the objectives of the finalization and attractiveness of the offer proposition.

From the cross between governance/regulation and MLP/SPT, four dials appear. Each dial represents a possible type of institutionalization of territorial policies. In the first dial (Dial 1), the institutionalization is of a legislative type. It describes a situation where the decision-making system is centralized and in charge of developing the laws and rules that apply to the whole territory.

In the second dial (Dial 2), the institutionalization is of a cultural type. Regarding the Bottom-Up approach, it starts from local issues and highlights emerging situations that can oppose or even contradict the Top-Down approach. The relationships between the Top-Down and Bottom-Up approaches described in the TVF must restore to decision-makers all the existing or future situations in which the different territorial actors find the technical and normative regime that allows them to concretize a territorial policy (Dial 3 and 4).

In the TVF, the MLP axis (Dial 1 and 2) gives rise to a process of monitoring the territory on the state of Bottom-Up and Top-Down practices. This watch serves as the basis for a territorial diagnosis and allows for understanding how these two dials establish pressure or even possible opposition in their relations between initiative and control. The TVF looks for the terms of this pressure or opposition in three forms of ability:

- An ability to extend: it focuses on generalizing all the content and benefits of joint action and globalizing access to goods deemed common. This ability seeks to favor the equality that the application provides to all rather than attention to the individual. It is also visible with the aim of retaining substantial and forward-looking challenges and sharing them across an entire territory. It expresses exemplary values that only make sense if they are addressed to all (the value of legitimacy and urgency by the stakeholders).

- An ability to understand: it is directly linked to the possession of the details of the action content and the context of its implementation. It expresses the details of a motivation that accompanies the experience of a specific need whose properties remain difficult to generalize as it stands. This ability to master the ins and outs of a particular proximity situation also serves as a driver for stakeholders' involvement based on customizable knowledge held and transmitted by the initiators of the action (the emergency value and perceived legitimacy by stakeholders)

-     A decision-making ability: it is essentially a power to influence or decide using means that the actors think they have or not. It supposes not only an appreciation of the actors' autonomy but also a capacity of judgment capable of making a compatible optimum of extension with an optimum of understanding (the value of the power of decision-making by the stakeholders).

Often the critical point of territorial policies is that a maximum effort of extension corresponds, by necessity, to a minimum effort of understanding and vice versa. It is, therefore, a question of finding the sustainable balance between the effort of extension and understanding efforts. Maintaining this critical point at an explainable and acceptable level by all stakeholders is posed by the TVF as one of the drivers of territorial dynamics. Associated with this critical point, the TVF puts forward the concepts of creation of potential and immediate result in the control of the territorial dynamics to be evaluated and animated. The creation of potential for a territory essentially consists in asking the question: what should decision-makers propose tomorrow to maintain the long-term attractiveness of the territory? The instantaneous result rather referring to the question: what must decision-makers do today to offer the promised uses? Usually, emergence and initiative refer to the creation of potential, the legislative and the normative to the demand for immediate results. In the TVF, development is an integrative process between the creation of potential and instant results that decision-makers are responsible for maintaining positive tension.

The following figure (figure 3.3) presents the specific nature of the efforts of extension and understanding according to the Bottom-up and Top-down approaches. In these two cases, the dynamics of territorial action are essentially from the efforts of extension and understanding at work in the so-called emerging modes of governance and regulation and in the modes of "sited" governance and regulation, depending on whether they are ascending or descending.

In the ascending ones, the dynamics of development finds its explanation in the existence among the actors of a will and a logic of their initiatives recognition. This recognition can be sought by the actors and considered a source of their satisfaction when it receives an institutional validation.

From the emerging local, these initiatives generally seek the normative and legislative of "sited" governance and regulation and the confirmation of their external validity and their generalizable character. In this ascending logic of promotion of initiatives, the effort of extension must be maximum. It tends to reduce the effort of understanding some generalizable elements below the objections concerning the particularity of emerging experiences. The emerging level must offer a global and globalizing approach that is able to impose itself as such up to a "sited" level. In response to this quest for the recognition of initiatives by the normative and legislative governance and regulation, the effort to understand "sited" governance and regulation must reach the maximum. It should integrate the dynamics resulting from the emerging level, and then evaluate what in these initiatives can be extended to general practices, a norm, a rule, and even a law.

With the Top-down approach, this dynamic is reversed, we move from a logic of recognition of heterogeneous initiatives to a logic of homogenization of practices applicable to all, namely, a logic of procedures guaranteeing these practices. The Top-down approach is driven by a requirement for submission and dissemination from the particular public interest to the general public interest. In the Top-down logic that intends to impose the content of law or rule, the effort of extension must be maximum and the effort of understanding should be reduced to what could be a major objection of applicability, in response to the law or standards in the name of the general interest or good practices. On the contrary, regulation must be at the maximum of understanding to avoid the quickly circumventing formalism of directives that are not applicable. This maximum of understanding must feed a form of jurisprudence and reinsurance. Local applications are thus framed and do not contravene the exercise and defense of the general interest.

Figure 3-3: The logic of extension and understanding in the Bottom-Up and Top-Down approaches

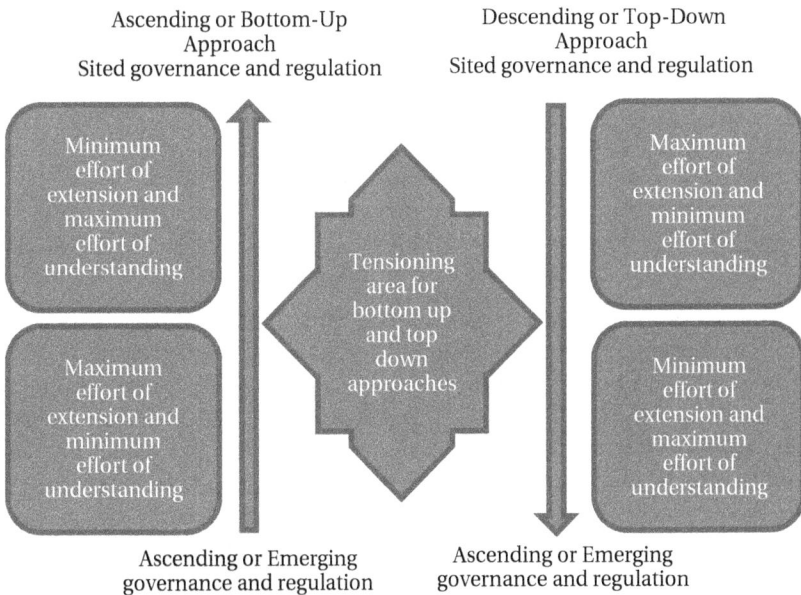

Ascending or Bottom-Up Approach
Sited governance and regulation

Descending or Top-Down Approach
Sited governance and regulation

Minimum effort of extension and maximum effort of understanding

Maximum effort of extension and minimum effort of understanding

Tensioning area for bottom up and top down approaches

Maximum effort of extension and minimum effort of understanding

Minimum effort of extension and maximum effort of understanding

Ascending or Emerging governance and regulation

Ascending or Emerging governance and regulation

It is in the context of optimization between extension, which defines the appropriate framework where standards and laws can apply, and understanding, which brings to life the diversity of the particular and leaves room for innovation, that decision-making capacity finds to practice. In the diagnosis, as in the development of the territory, the question of decision-making capacity essentially leads to that of the sharing of powers and the role that this sharing plays in the dynamics of territorial development.

The tension between the maximum extension that defines how far to extend the area covered by laws and standards and the maximum of understanding that seeks to capture the personal and civic motivations that drive societal practices is a key dimension of the interpretation of a territory and its development potential. Policymakers in this perspective are thus invited to ask, in particular, three questions that determine this interpretation:

- How are individual or group practices likely to contribute to the creation of potential observed, collected, supported, or encouraged in the territory?

- How do the legal or regulatory dimensions of these practices come into play? What do these dimensions offer to the organization and the dissemination of these practices? How do they meet the need for recognition? How can they be a recognition tool? What forms does the territory give to these dimensions to ensure a Bottom-up approach?

- How does the Top-down approach take adaptations from general to particular into account? What intermediation do they put in place to ensure these adaptations? And in this Top-down logic, are there forms of delegation or representation that allow actors to understand better the requirements of applying laws and standards to the territory?

- How do stakeholders perceive this tension? How are they affected? How should or should not they be associated with the resolution of these tensions, depending in particular on the urgency or legitimacy of their needs and the nature of their power?

In conclusion, the bottom-up and top-down approach, in terms of the tension between extension and understanding, gives meaning to the MLP axis. The latter is a useful indicator of the strategic room for maneuver for the autonomous functioning of a territory as well as its limits in terms of identity and autonomy. It is supplemented in the TVF by an operational approach resulting from the SPT that brings new perspectives on how to manage this room for maneuver. The SPT provides a technical approach to better deal with the tensions observed between extension and understanding in a territory.

The SPT axis falls within Dial 3 and 4 of figure 3.2. It represents the place and the engine from which the TVF develops all its capacity for interpretation and action. The SPT axis designs and organizes all the supports for action from which operators will be able to limit the MLP tensions presented in Dial 1 and 2 and to offer a balance favorable to the development between the efforts of extension and understanding across the territory.

These action supports can be thematic and draw on experience, expertise or memory and the past. They can also refer to the legislature exercise but in a delegated form that manages to adapt flexibly to the specificities of the territory, by seeking the local or regional conditions for the application of laws and regulations. The operators and these technical supports are responsible for creating acceptability and stability by ensuring the construction of references (benchmarks) and/or standards (cf. quality and so forth). Their construction is only possible by animating a monitoring system capable of observing the legislative constraints according to the territorial context. These benchmarks provide indicators of the evolution of these constraints and self-power the tension reduction system.

The first MLP axis defines the state of tension created by the question of the sharing of ascending and descending powers.

The second axis SPT attempts to stabilize this dynamic of conquest and power-sharing in an operational vision. This vision is conveyed in the search for rules or operating standards recognized and accepted by the stakeholders, who are capable of giving content and attractiveness to territorial offers. The challenges of the development dynamic captured by this MLP/SPT approach find their definitive interpretation in their appropriation by governance and regulation. This appropriation leads to a specific mode of stakeholders' integration in governance and the technical mastery of the content of attractive offers in regulation.

Within this framework of strategic analysis, the TVF, to read a situation or draw the most suitable paths of development, intends to be both holistic and integrative. Being holistic is because the TVF considers the future as the current or future resolution of a set of latent or overt tensions. Being integrative is to the degree that it associates the contents of the territorial offers and the attractiveness of their production modes including co-production, transfer, co-creation. These modes of production can only be conceived by the integration game of the various stakeholders. The TVF is part of a temporal dynamic. It adapts to each territorial context according to the relevance of the analyses it generates. The TVF also offers adapted support to evaluative logics by promoting questions and evaluation criteria based on the territorial system and its dynamics.

The TVF remains essentially a diagnostic and prospective tool thanks to which action plans can refine their presentation of a given territorial situation, find a consensus, and justify the strategic and operational options for the actions to be carried out. Besides, as a management tool, the TVF enables policymakers to characterize typical situations and generic modes of territorial development that can serve as so many references and facilitate the interpretative work.

3.2 The TVF and the modes of territorial development

The TVF, starting from the observation that a territory never lives in a vacuum, conceives of its development only in interaction with its geographic, institutional and political environment. To facilitate the interpretative work of a given territorial situation, the TVF proposes to characterize, with the concepts and tools that used, nine types or scenarios that allow revealing clearly differentiated territorial configurations. Each illustrates a particular situation and defines a specific profile based on four criteria:

- Criterion 1 (C1): *Governance and stakeholders*: the implementation of the territorial project implies a mode of governance that can be identified in particular by the nature and number of stakeholders that it integrates and by the institutional structures that it mobilizes.

- Criterion 2 (C2): *Regulation and combination of resources*: the implementation of the territorial project involves a regulation identifiable by technical and regulatory solutions that allow it to mobilize and combine various resources and to transform them according to the content of their offers and the means used to make them attractive.

- Criterion 3 (C3): *The ability to diversify the forms of value creation*: the territorial dynamic is dependent totally on the concept of value creation. This creation can be observed from the variety of modes of creation it requires, from the co-production of this value to all the mechanisms put in place for co-creation, facilitation, transfer, etc.

- Criterion 4 (C4): *The methods of resolution of the tension between the informal emergence and the sited institution*: to ensure the territorial dynamics, the technical and normative nature of the management modes of tensions between extension and understanding must be evaluated in their facilitation or obstacle mechanisms.

The following tables present the nine territorial scenarios resulting from the application of these four criteria. These cases represent the main scenarios at the source of the multiplicity of the situations observed. These cases provide the references from which the main territorial situations are read. The following scenarios can be presented in three main categories:

- Category 1: Cases without intermediation modalities (Case 1 to 4). In these cases, there is an imbalance in territorial decision-making that results in noted shortcomings that are the lack of participation and concerted actions, the lack of delegation, the lack of search for power-sharing, and the lack of strategic orientations thought by the territory or linked to development challenges inspired by the national and international context.

- Category 2: Cases, within the MLP's framework, take into account the construction of a real territorial strategy by articulating the Bottom-Up and the Top-Down (Case 5 to 7). In these cases, a search for balance and stability forms the basis of territorial policies. They result in the implementation of an intermediation system. The latter allows the development of participatory processes.

- Category 3: Cases, in the SPT's context, take into account intermediation procedures (Case 8 and 9). In these cases, a search for balance and stability forms the basis of territorial policies. They result in the establishment of a thematic, technical or political intermediation system. The latter allows the development of participatory processes, the establishment of delegation systems, and the construction of a real territorial strategy. However, the weight of the legislative framework remains important and dominant.

The following tables show these different situations. For each case, the different reading criteria (C1, C2, C3, and C4) are proposed.

Table 3-1: Typology from a territorial policy without intermediation modalities

Case 1: Autonomous and thematic territorial development	Case 2: Opportunist territorial development

Case 3:	Case 4:
Centralized territorial development of normative and legislative type	Specialized and centralized territorial development (non-delegated system)

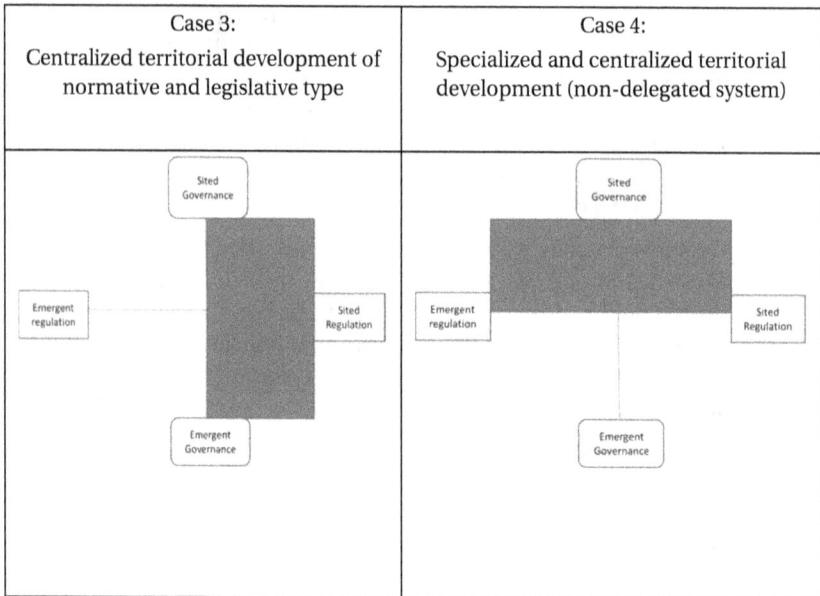

Case 1 describes territories that are very strongly anchored in a thematic dimension (e.g. the specialization of the territory's activities around know-how, the exploitation of a natural resource specifically owned or the enhancement of a historic heritage, etc.) whose development of the theme is not taken into account by the public authorities. Development is essentially emerging, giving way to local initiatives (regulation and emerging governance) in connection with the regulatory bodies ensuring the implementation of the theme (emerging regulation and sited governance). This scenario mainly materializes around the following dimensions:

Criterion 1: A thematic governance essentially brings together the actors related to the theme. A little intervention from public authorities often reduced to representation and public relations obligations.

Criterion 2: the strategic and operational choices about the offer proposition and its attractiveness rather than being carried by the thematic players without seeking regulation from the public or local authorities.

Criterion 3: the modes of value creation are not frozen. They call on co-production, often including the volunteering of actors interested in the theme, co-creation favored by the proximity of feedback, and in the culture of hosting initiatives, as well as in the transfer of value. Sometimes, the modes are based on the evocative character of the theme (tradition, recognized know-how, historical references, societal issues, etc.).

Criterion 4: The design and implementation of the offers and their dissemination do not involve the territory's regulatory systems. The regulation of an emerging nature, depending on local actors and actors external to the theme whose contributions become necessary for its development.

Case 2 designates especially the territories that do not present specific themes qualifying their activities. The combination of territorial resources is only completed if the opportunities arise in line with local initiatives or the impetus of the central authorities. These are territories that try to seize all the opportunities available without necessarily seeking the construction of comparative advantages that would synergistically call for privileged forms of development. From this point of view, the development strategy is based on the capacity to exploit contacts as they arise rather than to seek a long-term strategy of cumulative resources offering identifiable forms of territorial attractiveness in the long term. It is an opportunistic and diffuse development mode in which descendant stakeholders as well as ascendant must "make moves" in order to be seen as bearers of opportunity. The main dimensions are as follows:

Criterion 1: A centralized governance that expresses its determining role in the exercise of the capacity of contacts or influence turns towards the external stakeholders. It relies little on the delegation because it considers the territory unskilled to ensure its development effectively.

Criterion 2: A mode of regulation presents itself as the direct consequence of the conception of the selected development forms. For the sake of efficiency and responsiveness to the opportunities to be seized, the design and implementation of offers remain highly centralized to shorten the decision-making circuits and only to a limited number of stakeholders deemed competent and reactive in the interest of all.

Criterion 3: The modes of value creation are often those of the offer's producers. Co-production almost systematically refers to a divestiture of the ascendant in favor of the descendant when the initiative is appraised to have potential. Seizing opportunities creates forms of co-production that is often perceived as ineffective where the ascendant appears as a competitor and less well-placed to succeed if the descendant does not quickly oversee these initiatives. In this context, the value co-creation that requires renewed forms of collaboration and partnership withstand poorly Top-Down relationships on the lookout for opportunities that are quickly overlooked or rejected if they do not appear to have a significant effect deemed sufficient by the centralized bodies.

Criterion 4: The context that favors relational and networking opportunities makes secondary extension and understanding efforts as a development logic.

The understanding effort of the central authorities essentially comes down to the evaluation of initiatives on their ability to mobilize local actors in the short term on a scale deemed sufficient. The extension effort for these same actors refers only to their representativeness as interlocutors to the name of the territory. This tension, which has met with "immediate audibility" initiatives, is effective. It remains subject to the vagaries of a dialogue essentially oriented towards the external legibility of territorial projects, whatever they may be.

Case 3 describes territories that ensure their development without seeking to combine local resources with other resources. This is a false territorialization where the target territory is only the operational arm of the institutional territorial project. This case comes down to a purely Top-Down-oriented vision of territorial development. Territorial policy deploys the normative and legislative approach to the so-called "sited" institutional logic and completely omits the so-called emerging dimension. Case 3 reflects an interventionist approach to territorial development where local needs are subject to centralized interpretation. It is essentially characterized by the following dimensions:

Criterion 1: Centralized governance that relies on delegated structures to apply its guidelines and ensure their implementation.

Criterion 2: The strategic and operational choices concerning the offer proposition and its attractiveness are centralized. Moreover, operational implementation is delegated within the framework of a sited regulation.

Criterion 3: the modes of value creation come essentially from the offer producers. Co-production is just one element of delegated execution. The value co-creation given the nature of the modes of regulation is not sought as an essential element for the dynamics of development. The combination of resources is carried out by the definition thanks to fully sited regulation.

Criterion 4: In Case 3, the existence of any tension between the extension and understanding efforts is not formally conceivable. It does not lead to the strategic reflection of territory development. The extension effort is understood and at its maximum at the level of the players in the sited regulation. The understanding effort leaves little room for the particularities of local initiatives deemed a not particularly significant priori in the conduct of development.

Case 4 is specific to territories where the development strategy is explicitly oriented towards thematic specialization (territorial specificity). This orientation is the subject of a consensus that favors all the support linked to centralized and non-delegated actions. The combination of territorial resources is carried out in close interrelation between territorial governance bodies and thematic governance. This interrelation defines modes of collaboration with strongly sited governance. These are mainly territories that are managed according to imposed plans and those which leave little room for local initiatives.

Criterion 1: Governance organizes around the exploitation of a consensual theme. It brings together institutional and sited decision-makers in the territory with recognized and sited decision-makers on the theme.

Criterion 2: A highly centralized governance structure that chooses its interlocutors by recognizing them as representative of the thematic in an authoritarian relationship of non-delegated supervision.

Criterion 3: The main sources of value creation originate from the offer producers. Value co-production takes place only within the framework of a sited governance. It leaves little room for initiatives and the combination of resources can only be understood at the sited level.

Criterion 4: Ways to resolve the tension between the informal emergence and the sited institution are weak. The sited governance is characterized by a capacity of maximum extension, while the emerging governance remains in a situation of application and not of innovation.

Table 3-2: Typology from a Bottom-Up versus Top-Down dialectic (MLP axis)

Case 5: Autonomous and supported development (Bottom-up Vision)	Case 6: Territorial development from global governance	Case 7: Territorial development from global governance (Top-down Vision)

Case 5 takes the form of autonomous and supports territorial development. In this case, the progress takes place with the territory's resources. It is based on the enhancement of local potentials and specificities from local initiatives. The governance system supports local initiatives using thematic and technical support systems. In this situation, most of the territorial development devotes to local needs. Support for this type of development is inconceivable without solid links between local initiatives and thematic and normative support systems.

Criterion 1: A strongly emerging governance that is full of initiatives. It is characterized by an extension effort that attempts to formulate needs for the entire territory.

Criterion 2: A relatively weak mode of institutional intervention. It is motivated by a strong understanding effort to assume the specificities of emerging local needs and their expression.

Criterion 3: The modes of value creation in favor of co-production and co-creation. They strongly integrate into the development of local initiatives and positive externalities. Co-production and platforms to collect information from these externalities particularly solicit thematic and normative support systems and their resources.

Criterion 4: The weak modes of resolution of the tension between the informal emergence and the sited institutions. They are stabilized and accepted by a delegated and nature-agreed approach where the thematic and the normative governance present.

Case 6 is the so-called global governance. This governance attempts to combine the use of extra-territorial and territorial resources. The system of development that dominates here is the complementarity assumed of the Top-down and Bottom-up approaches. The territorial project is designed and implemented jointly by the territory, the partner territories and the centralized institutions. In the case of global governance, all the actors are in interaction with the definition and implementation of territorial policies. Territorial development is only conceivable if it places territorial needs in the continuity of extra-territorial orientations that these needs concretely decline as a contribution. In this case, the territorial policy adopts an institutional logic, both normative and legislative, while maintaining particular attention to territorial differentiation and the creation of potential stemming locally from emerging initiatives.

Criterion 1: Governance that seeks to associate, as inseparable partners, institutional representatives distributing extra-territorial resources and representatives of all stakeholders in the territory.

Criterion 2: A mode of intervention negotiated and built with all the actors involved by combining the resources necessary for territorial policy.

Criterion 3: A mode of value creation based on the co-production of global value and on the value co-creation thanks to the means offered, notably in information systems by global governance to develop all the potentials of the territory.

Criterion 4: The methods of resolving the tension between the informal emergence and the sited institutions are based on collective bargaining and participation. The maximum understanding of sited governance makes it possible to support emerging initiatives when they pay attention, at their maximum extension, and to express themselves at the local level as an extension of extra-territorial orientations.

Case 7: It Designates territories with a strong thematic specialization. The territorial policy is established on a search for specificities, sources of competitive advantages. The combination of resources is organized between the sited structures for governance and the regulation of the territory (centralized approach), the implementation of which is then delegated to thematic operators or territorial operators. This scenario adopts a Top-down type of territorial development vision relayed for thematic purposes by delegated operators.

Criterion 1: A moderately centralized governance and investment in the main theme to be exploited as a competitive advantage

Criterion 2: A Top-down type of intervention practicing thematic or normative delegation under the control of operating rules that set the limits of this delegation.

Criterion 3: A mode of value creation based on co-production where sited and centralized governance sets the standards and rules for combining resources. The value co-creation with thematic and normative delegations is fulfilled punctually on specific and limited missions.

Criterion 4: The tension between the informal emergence and the sited governance and sited regulatory structures finds its resolution between the maximum extension sought by these structures and the need for understanding necessary for delegated missions. Little room in this logic is left for local initiatives.

Table 3-3: Typology resulting from a territorial policy carried by an intermediation research (SPT axis)

Case 8: Delegated thematic territorial development.	Case 9: Delegated and not specialized territorial development

Case 8 presents territories mobilized at both emerging and sited levels by the search for a thematic affirmation. In fact, territorial strategies place a delegation to thematic and specialized operators at the center of this assertion. These operators are mainly responsible for ensuring the Bottom-up/Top-down dynamics between emerging initiatives and the sited governance and regulatory structures. They are entrusted with consolidating the theme and defining real competitive advantages as part of a territorial marketing approach. The combination of both emerging and sited resources contributes to the construction of the theme. It is delegated to an organization specialized in the management of this theme.

Criterion 1: A thematic delegated governance.

Criterion 2: A delegated mode of intervention, for the benefit of a Bottom-up institutional structure specializing in the theme carried by the territory.

Criterion 3: A value co-production/co-creation which attempts to combine resources in a thematic framework.

Criterion 4: A tension between emerging initiatives along with the sited governance and regulatory structures, relieved by the thematic delegation.

Case 9 highlights the case of territories whose development takes place in the light of a delegated normative approach. These are territories that follow conventional management and where initiatives are taken into account according to their nature by delegated bodies who are in charge of delegated management. Also, it is their responsibility to syndicate the territorial resources according to their areas of delegation (e.g., employment, economy, social, sustainable development, etc.).

Criterion 1: A governance based on the classic foundations of territorial management.

Criterion 2: A negotiated mode of intervention, intermediation done by delegated management structures

Criterion 3: A value co-production/co-creation that allows a combination of resources through delegated organizations.

Criterion 4: The tension between the informal emergence as well as the sited governance and regulatory structures is eased by the process of normative delegation. The latter allows development initiatives to be taken into account if these meet the concerns of the territorial management bodies.

Based on the criteria of the TVF, these nine cases represent the major and perfectly differentiated forms of territories that analysts and decision-makers may encounter. However, it depends on these analysts and decision-makers to be able to identify the salient characteristics of all these cases by disentangling them from their regularly more complex territorial context where their concrete form most often takes a mixed form.

The first function of these nine cases is to help characterize the existing situation of a territory. Beyond this function, in the phase of choosing the objectives of the action plan, the decision-maker should not only be able to find the scenario that best describes the territory, but also to specify, in the prospective plan, the case of figure towards which these objectives lead the territory. Each of these cases can synchronically be considered as a moment in the advancement of the territory. The TVF allows this synchronous reading by breaking down the evolutions of the territory into many characteristic moments. On the diachronic level, the temporal consideration of the sequence of these moments allows to construct or reconstruct the real or desired trajectory of a territory. Such an approach favors a critical view to contingent or competing elements that could blur the expected sequence.

The TVF does not provide a normative vision in territorial development strategies but offers an operational framework for analyzing different territorial situations. Territorial decision-makers can seize it to develop their strategy from an identified situation to go towards the desired situation. The TVF also helps to compare the different developments in the territories and to draw lessons from them in terms of forecasting.

In its analysis of the nine different territorial development situations, the TVF, in addition to the approaches presented above, essentially relies on two key elements that help to characterize the specific dynamics of each situation. The first element deals with the stakeholders involved in this dynamic, their place, their role, and the relationships they maintain. The second is related to the modes of production of value, by which the development dynamic is expressed in terms of attractiveness and mainly leads to value propositions made to the beneficiaries of action plans.

In chapters 4 and 5, these two elements will be detailed as tool 2- the stakeholders - and tool 3- the Cube Service Value (CSV)-. As complementary tools, they provide decision-makers with an optimal use of the TVF for the diagnosis and for the choice of the objectives of future territorial plans.

Bibliography

Hargreaves, T. Haxeltime, A. Longhurst, N. and Seyfang, G. 2011. "Sustainability transitions from the bottom up: civil society, the multi-level perspective and practice theory." Working Paper, *CSERGE*, n°1.

Mariam, Y. 1997. Proceeding of the 90th AW&MA meeting, Toronto.

Mariam, Y. 2007. "Environmental Sustainability and regulation: Top-down versus Bottom-un regulation." *MPRA*, paper n°413.

Vaesken, P. and Zafiropoulou, M. 2008a. "Les parties prenantes dans l'articulation de la régulation et de la gouvernance d'un territoire d'économie sociale et solidaire." *Colloque de l'AGRH*, Dakar Sénégal (Novembre).

Vaesken, P. and Zafiropoulou, M. 2008b. "Economie Sociale: une pratique de régulation territoriale." *Working paper* 5 CIRIEC.

Vaesken, P. 2012. "Régulation / Gouvernance en économie sociale et solidaire: un modèle pour comprendre l'innovation sociale territoriale." In *Administration de proximité et cohésion sociale*, edited by A Zanane. Rabat: Université Mohammed V.

Chapter 4

Method and Tool 2:
The Stakeholders Analysis

4.1 Tool 2: The analysis of stakeholders

To refine the capabilities of the Territorial Value Framework (TVF) to grasp a territorial development situation, stakeholder analysis is inescapable. In the presentation of this Tool 2, the analysis is principally devoted to the capacities of territorial actors to combine their resources to produce or benefit from an offer proposition.

Freeman (1984, 2010), founding father of the stakeholder theory, offers a general analysis which, in the present case, remains relevant for making a first approach to the places and roles of stakeholders within an organization. Any actor, according to Freeman, who shares a positive or negative interest with the territorial project, is considered a stakeholder.

Stakeholders are thus directly involved in the dynamics of the development of a territory and the estimation of its potentials. They are generally defined by the fact of issuing an offer or a demand that corresponds to the objectives of the territorial entities and their public or private partners (Freeman and Reed 1983; Hill and Jones, 1992), or by the meaning that they give to the action of these same entities (Wicks et al, 1994). Their modes of engagement can be varied. Clarkson (1994) even advances the idea that a stakeholder is not necessarily in a current relationship with the actors of the plan and gains its status by mere potentiality as a "latent stakeholder". Such a possible extension of stakeholder status requires that policymakers have useful concepts to understand the multiplicity of places and roles that these stakeholders can occupy in a developing territory.

These places and roles are even more varied and difficult to grasp since they can address potentially beneficial stakeholders. Their places and roles do not correspond directly to a legal, normative, or cultural mission. They are based on their value judgments and their perception of the attractiveness of the action plan's offer propositions. Stakeholders can act either spontaneously, voluntarily and purposefully, or in an imposed and prescribed manner. This multifaceted commitment is associated with purely territorial issues including offers acceptation, or with external missions affecting the territory. The analysis of the commitments addresses these dynamics from the essential point of view of the resources they involve. The places and roles thus described can be read from the actors of the resources combination at work in all forms taken by the MLP (Multi-Level-Practices) and by the SPT (Social Practices Theory) depending on whether these stakeholders represent legal (in the principle of authority), emerging (in cultural principle), or even normative (technical or political) institutions.

These places and these roles give rise to relatively successful resources combination, where co-productions and co-creations, concerted procedures, partnerships, cooperation, relatively formal alliances, and spontaneous mutualization are observed. The analysis developed in this presentation of Tool 2 completes that of Freeman (1984, 2010), taking inspiration in particular from the typology of actors proposed by Mitchell et Al. (1997). This typology introduces a new dimension to the dynamics of development in addition to the power and legitimacy proposed by Freeman (1984): that of the urgency of the action to be undertaken. These three dimensions provide means of useful interpretation for the TVF to tackle the dynamics of territorial development.

4.2 Stakeholder analysis, what reading grid for the analysis of territorial development?

In the application of the TVF, stakeholder analysis is essential to assess territorial dynamics. Originally, Freeman's analysis, within the framework of the theory of organizations, defined the companies' operating methods as an arrangement of the various stakeholders. These modalities extend perfectly to the territory.

In this case, it is necessary to identify how the stakeholders in a territory build their relationships and make them evolve in organizations or progress individually and collectively in the conduct of territorial policies. Figure 4.1 below makes it possible to interrelate three main categories of stakeholders characterized by two dimensions: power and legitimacy. Power, for actors, corresponds to the expressed or potential capacity of influencing or making the decisions. The legitimacy of the actors comes from their missions or their implications in an action that gives them a right of scrutiny, participation, or even veto over the decision.

The intersection (figure 4-1) of these two spheres reveals the so-called "essential" or decision-making stakeholders, who ensure the governance and regulation of a project or an organization. These actors are at the heart of the territorial dynamic. The grid proposed by Freeman remains relevant in simple and stable economic and political environments. The reality is often very different and much more complex.

Figure 4-1: Freeman's Stakeholder Analysis Model (1984)

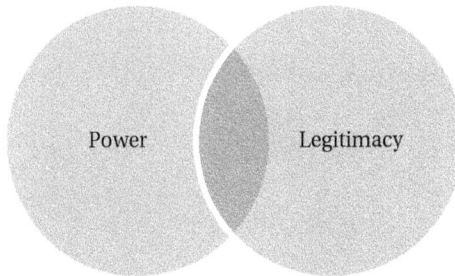

The question then becomes: What are the specific traits of the stakeholders that best show their different places and roles in the dynamics of territorial development? How to relate a given state of territorial development to the modes of the stakeholders' action, to their behavior of initiatives or that of adversity to the changes? How to assess, given this state, the development potentials of a territory and the means of influence to be deployed to act on the attitudes and behaviors of these stakeholders? These questions refer policymakers to that of identifying the most significant profiles of these stakeholders regarding their capability of getting involved or not with the territorial development process, and their ability to motivate themselves to act or not depending on their judgment on the offer propositions. Thus, other variables used to characterize the profiles of stakeholders are essential to the interpretive and prospective work of the TVF, both to make the diagnosis and to drive territorial development.

To achieve this objective, Freeman's proposal to retain power and legitimacy as variables for identifying stakeholders appears obvious but insufficient. In effect, it brings together experts and decision-makers as key stakeholders. A third variable offers a parsimonious and useful means of differentiating the places and roles of stakeholders and especially those concerning the beneficiaries of territorial action. This variable is urgency. Mitchell, Agle and Wood (1997) introduce a dimension complementary to those of power and legitimacy. The urgency defines the degree of the actors' sensitivity to the needs for which the territorial development plan seeks to respond. It characterizes a chronic requirement of the stakeholders, which can be a demand or a need considered fundamental and to be satisfied in the short term.

The authors, after Freeman, thus cross the three added variables. This crossover reveals eight types of stakeholders.

The intersections of Figure 4.2 differentiate the stakeholders in the following way:

Figure 4-2: Mitchell, Agle and Wood's Stakeholder Analysis Model (1997)

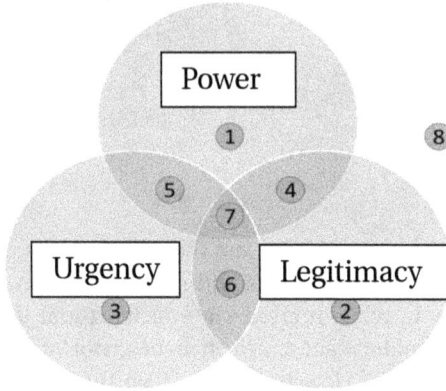

Regarding stakeholders who fall under one of the three dimensions. These stakeholders only participate indirectly in the resources combination necessary for the offer proposition. They can support or contribute to the resources transformation, benefit from the offer without necessarily being the recipients or the users. These stakeholders cannot play the role of "prior integrator" (Vargo and Lusch 2004), that is to say, the role of driving and coordinating the combination and the value creation. These stakeholders illustrate particular relationships with value creation that policymakers must beware of neglecting in their assessment of development dynamics. These stakeholders, while not being at the heart of territorial development, can contribute significantly by creating contextual value (Vargo 2008). This form of value refers to the fact that the beneficiaries can profit from the value without the direct use of the offer thanks to indirect interactions such as imagination, reputation, recommendations, and prescriptions. These stakeholders, in a given social and spatial context, can co-create symbols or meanings that contribute indirectly to the directions of development.

These stakeholders are defined according to the three variables selected as follows:

-1- Dormant stakeholders: this status is granted to actors who can exert a strong influence, but who are not in a position to create values in use, deemed urgent and legitimate for the transformation of the territory. The peculiarity of these dormant stakeholders is that they only have to develop another dimension (legitimacy or urgency) so that the opportunity to interact directly with them or to integrate their resources into the development dynamic appears.

-2- Discretionary stakeholders: this status is granted to stakeholders who, alongside development actions, create values in use that can be regarded as legitimate in the territory. They cannot claim any urgency and do not exercise any particular power. These marginal stakeholders, if their legitimacy is recognized, may change their status in crisis or transition situations linked to changes in the assessment of the mode of development.

-3- Demanding stakeholders: This status is granted to stakeholders who claim access to values in use in the name of urgency but without having a strong influence on the objectives of territorial transformation, nor acquired any real legitimacy to claim it. They appear capable of scrambling the merits of the policies pursued without being able to question them. The answers to the illegitimacy of their requirements can be occasions to recall the priorities of the action plan and the values in use that it promotes.

Regarding the stakeholders who fall under two of the three dimensions, it highlights the problem of legitimacy or urgency with or without the holding of power. This category brings stakeholders together whose interactions or commitments are particularly unstable. These stakeholders are defined as follows:

-4- Dominant stakeholders: This status is assigned to stakeholders who hold both legitimacy and power in formulating and implementing the transformation objectives. They are lobby groups that matter and have views on what values in use to offer and how to offer. The recognition of their status by governance can advantageously go through formalization (such as partnership agreement, contractualization, quotation as referent, etc.). The analysis of the organization of their lobby group is useful. It should lead to propositions for the integration and combination of their own resources in the production of offers (e.g., the committee of experts, study days, ad-hoc study commissions, seats on governance boards, and consultations on regulatory actions).

-5- Dangerous stakeholders: This status is granted to stakeholders who assert strong influence and the urgency of their request without being able to claim any legitimacy concerning territorial objectives. The power of this type of stakeholder is neither institutional nor truly societal. It is based on the search for imposition, a balance of power that can be based on threat, blackmail or even violence when its illegitimate character is particularly manifest. It is necessary to reinforce the illegitimate character of this stakeholder by denouncing his way of wanting to exercise power.

-6- Dependent stakeholders: This status is granted to stakeholders who have little influence over the transformation process, but submit a perfectly legitimate and urgent request for use in relation to the providers' objectives. The governance and regulation of the providers have to be exercised through acting as their spokesperson or promoting relays with other dominant stakeholders. Providers can officially recognize dependent stakeholders' requests by giving them full places in existing objectives or in objectives to be formulated. Depending on the degree of legitimacy and urgency of the requests, the governance and regulation of the providers can help to strengthen the power of this stakeholder deemed to be illustrative of the values in use to be promoted.

Concerning the stakeholders who present the three dimensions, in this context, the stakeholders can combine all the resources carried by each category of stakeholders in order to build an offer proposition.

-7- Decisive stakeholders: This status is granted to stakeholders who combine power, legitimacy and urgency. They are best positioned to lead governance and regulation in order to achieve their objectives or meet their expectations. To boost territorial development, these stakeholders must interact and collaborate with other legitimate stakeholders. They can set priorities when they recognize urgency. They must also negotiate with the dominant stakeholders who have the power over not to remain inactive and to be heard. Likewise, they must be particularly sensitive to dormant stakeholders, who are important contributors to brand image and/or reputation that are vehicles of symbolic values in building the attractiveness of the territory and its offers. Finally, these decisive stakeholders must be particularly attentive to the creation of potentials, innovation and the emergence that the propositions of discretionary stakeholders may contain. Likewise, they must also act as spokespersons for dependent stakeholders in order to maintain consistency in development and to judge the threat posed by demanding or dangerous stakeholders to this territorial consistency.

-8- Non stakeholders: This status is assigned to all those who do not fit in any of the three proposed dimensions. They appear far removed from territorial development. However, this status may change if active stakeholders come to give them, at the border with dormant stakeholders, possible influence.

Table 4-1: Summary of the stakeholders' characteristics

Type of stakeholders	Dimension	Possible roles in development	Description and importance in development
Dormant	Power	Source of potential	The stakeholder has power to influence, but does not have legitimacy and cannot invoke urgency. The reality of its power has to be recognized to become effective.
Discretionary	Legitimacy	Source of potential	The stakeholder has legitimacy, but has neither the power nor the ability to exert immediate pressure in the name of the urgency. Recognition of their legitimacy can be a source of emerging development and innovation.
Demanding	Urgency		The stakeholder claims only urgency, without power or legitimacy. Its recognition requires a selection of claims so as not to deviate from the territorial development objectives.
Dominant	Power Legitimacy	Source of tension	The stakeholder has power and legitimacy. His recognition is equivalent to the introduction into governance and regulation of actor with whom power-sharing will have to be negotiated.
Dependent	Legitimacy Urgency	Source of tension	The stakeholder has legitimacy, reinforced by the urgency. Its recognition can be a factor of development coherence and avoids creating "left behind".
Dangerous	Power Urgency		The stakeholder has mainly a power of a coercive nature or an opposition on the merits of the action. His recognition in the event of loss of power can be dangerous for the proposed action.
Decisive	Power Legitimacy Urgency	Decision-Making	The stakeholder has both power and legitimacy. He exercises a major responsibility. Among these responsibilities, there is that of knowing how to combine its resources with all those of stakeholders who can in different ways contribute to the optimum transformation of the territory.

This typology of stakeholders has an interest that should be emphasized. It tries to avoid the dangers of the undifferentiation of actors and beneficiaries in the face of development issues. It completes the classical segmentation resulting from economic or socio-demographic variables by three main dimensions of the development dynamic. The use of this typology proposed above requires that the developing territory viewed as the places where the stakeholders' resources can be combined to transform them. In this sense, planning for development amounts to organizing and strategically combining the variety of resources of the different types of stakeholders in order to optimize territorial transformation.

The nature of the resources proposed by the stakeholders and how they combine those resources form the basis of the TVF's conception of territorial dynamics. Territorial development strategies question the resources they must mobilize. They provide the incentives capable of leading to their combination and integration, according to the resources and the type of stakeholders who hold them. The typology in this approach is operational on two conditions:

-Define the stakeholder(s) best positioned to take the initiatives to coordinate the combination and thus become the "prime resources integrators" (Moeller 2008) of the transformation. In understanding the territorial dynamics, these questions of taking the initiatives or the responsibility for coordinating one or more stakeholders are relayed by those of the participation and collaboration of other stakeholders, particularly in the co-production and co-creation of values. The dynamic of the territory is assured more since the stakeholders involved in the territorial transformation can take the roles of "prime resources integrators" notably in the values co-creation. This role of "prime resources integrator" can be exercised without necessarily depending on any legal or normative coercive power.

-Place as explicitly as possible the nature and the mode of value creation expected from this combination and ensure the power of motivation or attractiveness of these values if they are potential, in exchange or in use.

When these two conditions are satisfied, the governance takes the initiatives, solicits the stakeholders, calls on their resources, and adapts them to the mode of combination and value creation that will lead to the offer of development.

This approach thus enables the management of the combination and integration of stakeholder's resources, ranging from the most emerging ones to the most organized and formalized ones, according to the offer proposition and the types of stakeholders involved. In terms of regulation, it precisely guides the content of the transformation. The regulation adapts the content of the offer proposition according to the evolution of the stakeholders, particularly their values in use and the appearance of externalities linked to these uses.

By associating power, legitimacy and urgency with these two conditions of initiatives and value creation, this approach can help to qualify the specific dynamics of territory. They reveal the concrete elements on which this dynamic can be optimized.

This approach of stakeholders in a territory, where the modes of combining stakeholders' resources are privileged, has a significant consequence. Territorial development policy appears to be a node of sought-after interdependencies where all actors can alternatively play the role of prior integrator depending on the value creation modes chosen and deemed the most conducive to development.

To succeed in such a policy, the TVF adds two additional variables to complete the analysis: the MLP and the SPT. For the MLP, the level of tension to be negotiated between initiatives and controls, attempts to make the maximum extension efforts compatible with the necessary understanding. For the SPT, the nature of the technical regime capable of obtaining a consensus among the stakeholders on concrete solutions finalizes the offer propositions and promotes their attractiveness and acceptability. The respect of these two variables in the TVF defines the capacity for decision. The appreciation of a territorial development policy or its construction is achieved as both obtaining immediate results and creating the potentials for development.

In the TVF, the MLP looks at the tensions between understanding and extension by putting the emergent and the sited face to face, which is the maximum effort of extension and the minimum effort of understanding. The logic behind this "tension" is that of the opposition between the search for recognition and the obligation to respect the rules or the law. In this logic, the opposition that the "integrators of primary resources" have to settle is that of the advance, towards the desired generalization of practices which leads the extension effort to its maximum.

From this point of view, on the contrary, the TVF considers the search for the technical regime of the SPT in a logic that is turned entirely towards practical success and adaptation to the individuals' data[1]. In this logic, it is the effort of understanding that is thus at its maximum.

4.3 Stakeholders, territorial policies and TVF

The acknowledgement of actors in the construction of territorial policies, therefore, falls within the first framework, a legal framework. Sited stakeholders

---

[1] Figure 3.3 summarizes this situation where the MLP seeks between the emergent and the situated the maximum of extension, and the SPT seeks on the same opposition the maximum of understanding.

who represent the law or demand to legislate based on new facts and/or stakeholders who invest with territorial or extraterritorial missions are trying to negotiate. They negotiate in particular to reduce tensions with the various actors, normally carrying emerging practices, innovation, and initiatives that try to settle in the territory by seeking the maximum extension.

This consideration also finds a normative framework. Sited or emerging stakeholders seek the technical regime in which by a delegation of the legal framework, the development propositions find their concrete content in an agile and comprehensive manner or for the sake of adaptation. This technical regime is concerned with practical success, whether it depends on a delegation of the legal framework, or depends on associations and groups raising normative or technical obstacles on the ground for the only stakeholders concerned. This regime is negotiated to respect a maximum of understanding perceived as a success factor. These two frameworks, legal and normative, delimit the problems of the MLP and the SPT respectively.

The approach, at each stage of the analysis proposed above, examines how the stakeholders can contribute to the development of the territory according to their power, their legitimacy or the urgency of their situation. This contribution continues depending on whether they naturally play an important but not exclusive role of "prime resources integrators", or whether they engage in a process of value creation according to their resources. There are useful perspectives on the relationships that stakeholders can maintain.

These dynamic effects depend mainly on the ability of stakeholders to resolve tensions or obtain concrete results through efforts to adapt their technical regime. Updating them helps to refine the contribution of stakeholders to territorial dynamics. However, the issue of stakeholders' interaction capacities and that of the cumulative effects of their practices on the territory deserve to be clarified. The objective is to obtain a synthetic vision of the territory and the dynamics of its development. Inspired by Freeman (1984), Mitchell, Agle and Wood (1997) and Pallemaerts and Moreau (2004), the TVF offers a synthetic view of this dynamic. It consists of breaking down this dynamic into seven distinct dynamics, noting its presence and, possibly, its absence, and then examining its positive or negative contribution to the overall dynamic. Each development dynamic is supported by a relational function through which the stakeholders interact.

The state of the relational function of a dynamic indicates the overall dynamics of a territory. The observation of this function, where relatively complex interactions are exerted, and their effects help to recompose the dynamics of development to arrive at a global synthesis. Figure 4.3 suggests locating each of the development dynamics from the first three variables chosen by the TVF and inspired by Freeman (1984) and Mitchell, Agle and Wood

(1997). This localization is based on the principle that power, legitimacy and urgency are at the root of the behavior of territorial stakeholders. They are the necessary but not sufficient conditions for understanding their interactions by which all territorial policy is constructed.

Figure 4.3 shows that this general dynamic can firstly be understood as a "given state of interrelations" among these three necessary conditions. The absence of interrelationships for a function in a territory reflects the weakness of this development dynamic. In the first phase of the analysis, Figure 4.3 shows that the different dynamics may depend merely on one of these necessary conditions, which is the case. For example, the dynamic of a decision can link to power, that of legitimacy linked to legitimacy and that of alert to the urgency. The dynamics may alternatively depend on basic interrelations, such as the dynamic of expertise linked to power and legitimacy, opposition to power and emergency, awareness and education to legitimacy and urgency, and governance to power, legitimacy and urgency.

Figure 4-3: The dynamics of territorial development

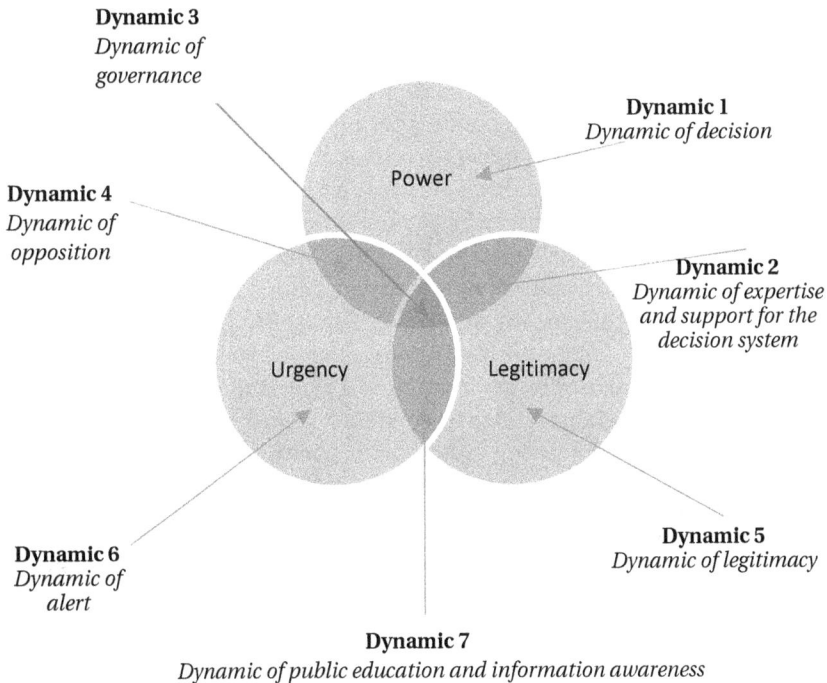

Dynamic 3
Dynamic of governance

Dynamic 1
Dynamic of decision

Dynamic 4
Dynamic of opposition

Power

Dynamic 2
Dynamic of expertise and support for the decision system

Urgency

Legitimacy

Dynamic 5
Dynamic of legitimacy

Dynamic 6
Dynamic of alert

Dynamic 7
Dynamic of public education and information awareness

Each of these seven dynamics refers to a specific definition. It is accompanied by a basic relational function such as, a power that can be exercised in isolation by all the stakeholders who have it (even though the interrelations may be absent) or be performed in a more complex function if this power is shared, especially, with stakeholders who do not directly possess it. For some of these dynamics, their fundamental relational function involves interrelations. It is the case with governance that can only be fully exercised when power, legitimacy and urgency interact among the involved stakeholders. Again, in its complex forms, the stakeholders do not necessarily hold the complete relational function composed of power, legitimacy and urgency, but can enter into dynamics with those who hold it.

Such a configuration, in complex expressions, can be far from this fundamental relational function. It reveals logic of communication, consultation, collaboration, and even sharing of governance with stakeholders who do not hold all the complete function. The TVF, according to the relatively complex forms that the dynamics take and their respective relational function seeks to interpret: how each dynamic contributes or not to the overall dynamic of territorial development.

The TVF retains seven dynamics designating the vital forms of the dynamics of territorial development:

-Dynamic 1- the dynamic of decision. This dynamic, to be fully exercised, requires power, legitimacy, and the capacity to react to the urgency. From this point of view, territorial development is essentially dependent on the so-called "decisive stakeholders". Contextual elements and, in particular, those related to the pressure of the urgency can help analysts to measure if the fundamental relational function is actually exercised. It will be necessary to observe whether this dynamic develops a more complex relational function in decision-making depending on the problems to be solved. Attention can be drawn to how the relational function integrates decision-making by stakeholders, such as dominant stakeholders who are legitimate and powerful and seek power-sharing for more legitimacy in decisions and meaning in power practice. Likewise, the relational function at stake here involves all the participatory or concerted approaches proposed by this dynamic, such as by empowering stakeholders who do not have power.

-Dynamic 2- the dynamic of expertise and support for the decision system. This dynamic is a key element of the territory's development strategy. It reveals or not the capacity of the decision-making dynamic to surround itself with enlightening advice in internal or external resources. The relational function implemented in this dynamic comes from listening and influencing relationships that it can create. The construction of the legitimacy of the decision is likely to rely on it. The relational function of this dynamic is often complex insofar as all stakeholders seeking legitimacy and power can use it. This dynamic is at the heart of the relationships between the dynamic of decision-making, that of governance, opposition, and even alert (for demanding stakeholders) when stakeholders use them to strengthen their power and legitimacy. The ability of this dynamic to develop knowledge and opinions, the sources of power and legitimacy, fuels all the relational functions of other dynamics and contributes to a synthetic view of the dynamics of territory development.

-Dynamic 3- the dynamic of governance. This dynamic depends on its basic relational function on the three conditions of power, legitimacy and urgency. It, therefore, appears like the one that can have the most complex and abundant relational function. It is the leading place of negotiation and partnership. It thus opens, for the TVF, important possibilities for interactions between stakeholders and particularly those who do not have all the dimensions of the relational function of governance. In a certain context of seeking consensus on large development projects or on projects that offer easy and common ground, favorable to development, the relational function of governance held by decision-makers, even dominant stakeholders, can be extended voluntarily to so-called "opposition stakeholders". The decision-makers can give them access to the complete relational function for moments of chosen and shared governance. The analysts thus can see concretely where a territory is in the establishment of these relationships. The analysis relates to how the MLP adjusts the tensions between the emerging and the sited and where the SPT does not exclude the technical regime any proposal or solution coming from all actors including the demanding actors and, under certain conditions, the dangerous ones.

-Dynamic 4- The dynamic of opposition. This dynamic is based on power and urgency, but, above all, on questioning the legitimacy of the proposals from governance. It is an excellent indicator of the development prospects of a territory. Access to the full relational function of the dynamic of opposition requires negotiation with the dynamic of existing governance. It thus gives a fair idea of the state of territory mobilization and that of its capacity to negotiate in a dynamic of governance that knows how to exploit all the possibilities of its relational function.

-Dynamics 5- The dynamic of legitimation. This dynamic is based on a fundamental relational function subject to a single condition: legitimacy. It illustrates the normative and cultural aspects of the institutional and historical sources of legitimacy in a territory. Discretionary stakeholders represent well the historical and cultural legitimacy that sometimes finds it difficult to gain recognition. The interest of the observer is to distinguish between this legal or acquired legitimacy and legitimacy to be conquered. To build and impose themselves, discretionary stakeholders must interact with other development dynamics. It is particularly interesting to observe the produced interactions and the dynamics involved in a territory in order to gain legitimate status. Thus, in most cases, the dynamic of legitimacy seeks to interact with expertise. The construction of this legitimacy and its acquisition also lead to interactions with the so-called dynamic of public education and information awareness. In this case, the ability to build arguments and disseminate them can serve as an index to the efforts of stakeholders seeking legitimacy. The relational function of legitimacy is a powerful indicator of the capacity of a territory to strengthen the MLP. It resolves the tensions between the emerging and the sited when the stakeholders who hold power and legitimacy are satisfied through recognition in legitimacy, the maximum effort to extend Bottom-Up initiatives. The analysis of the relational function of the dynamics of legitimacy is, therefore, one of the crucial elements of the general analysis of the dynamics of territory development. Legitimacy is also, in this logic of recognition, an essential tool for opening up the dynamic of decision and governance to the various stakeholders holding a dynamic of opposition or even an alert.

-Dynamics 6- The dynamic of alert. This dynamic is by nature of anticipation and vigilance shared by all stakeholders in a territory, including the dormant ones. In the general problems of territorial development, this dynamic is fundamental to bring about the necessary changes in all aspects of everyday life in the territory. The observation of the importance or not of the relational function of this dynamic is an interesting indicator of the stakeholders' vigilance associated with the dynamics of decision or governance or even the dynamics of opposition. This vigilance supposes that the alert dynamic benefits from a process capable of enriching its basic relational function. This process, enshrined in the MLP, is that governance ensures the least possible tension between extension and understanding to anticipate the consequences of the alert and provide the most suited responses to the scale of the urgency. The relational function of the alert dynamic should be able to interact with expertise, and support for the decision system, public education and information awareness in order to interact with the parties according to the emergency stakeholders who have the power and the legitimacy and, therefore, have the capacity to intervene. This process, which extends the relational function of alert, reactivates the need for legitimacy recognition of the urgency. This relational function is the only one capable of ensuring the maximum extension to a Bottom-Up alert.

-Dynamic 7- The dynamic of public education and information awareness. This dynamic is essential to activate the significant development behaviors associated with the necessary but not sufficient conditions of power, legitimacy and urgency. This dynamic cannot exist if its relational function is not in interaction with an alert, making the freedom to inform the first prerequisite. A second prerequisite is the code of ethics for the collection of communication and teaching information content. The diagnosis in a territory of this dynamic relational function, in particular with the decisive or dominant stakeholders or with those who drive the dynamic of opposition, is determining the future of the conduct of development.

The presentation of these seven dynamics of territorial development and their respective relational function should facilitate general appreciations of the development of each territory. This presentation provides the main lines of an assessment that only concrete analysis can approach. These broad lines depend on the observation of presence or absence in a territory of these seven dynamics. The observation, then, extends to the dynamics which can be observed in the way that each one maintains or not a relational function beyond the fundamental functions describing the elementary relationships among power, legitimacy and urgency.

According to the TVF, all the relationships that express the possible complexity of each dynamic relational function must give an overview of how a territory masters by its governance the negotiation stakes of the MLP and combines by its regulation in the SPT stakeholders' resources involved in technical regimes leading to development offers.

In all development strategies, from firms to territories, it is clear that it is impossible to create a priori development model that guarantees the success of the territory in all circumstances. If the TVF cannot draw universal lessons on how to conduct territorial development, it does intend to reveal how certain states of development and their relational function reveal obstacles to progress. The policymakers must correct them due to the numerous weaknesses. Conversely, the TVF can try to reveal success factors in a territory linked to some of these states, disclosing the game among the stakeholders concerned by the development of the territory.

To make possible syntheses on the development dynamics of a territory, the TVF proposes to compare a given state of the different development dynamics and their relational functions with two key variables that describe two critical capacities of the territory's stakeholders. These capacities are better mastered as they mobilize a large number of development dynamics in the understanding of the future of the territory. The first deals with the ability to perceive the evolution of the environment (reactivity) or to identify exploitable opportunities for the territory (proactivity).

It emphasizes the collective capacity of the territory to define a future. It highlights the dynamics of development and the relational functions that the territory can mobilize to interpret its future and make it known in concrete terms. In this context, it is, above all, the dynamics of decision, expertise, governance, and communication that are directly inspected. This first variable essentially targets the analytical and prospective capacities of decisive and dominant stakeholders, like "prime resources integrators" and all those concerned with expertise and communication.

However, the strength of the interpretation and the search for a possible consensus push analysts to examine how the relational functions of these dynamics extend or not to other dynamics and stakeholders. The dynamic of governance contributes directly to the evaluation of this variable. It is the MLP and its ability to bring the Bottom-up and Top-down to life that is concerned at this point. Analysts can look for a clear indication of this dynamic in the interest it carries and the follow-up it gives to all Bottom-up propositions. The emerging place in the definition of the territory's future thus becomes one of the expressions of this governance dynamic and the adapted nature of its relational function.

The second variable touches on the ability to trigger change processes (reactive or proactive) and to designate partners and the resources to enforce them. The second variable allows including in the assessment of the development dynamic and primarily the dynamics of opposition, legitimacy, and alert. The other dynamics of capacity 1 are always indispensable for the evaluation, but the capacity to prompt changes and to propose new or even substitute technical regimes gives dynamics 4, 5 and 6 a role which can be pivotal in the discussion on the effective territory regulation.

Dynamics, especially when their relational functions are consistent and go beyond basic functions, have their places and roles when it comes to refining the technical regimes that build the offers of the territory. The attractiveness of their propositions can be the source of a desire for change when, in particular, these propositions designate the partners and the combinations of resources to bring them fruition. It is clear, however, that the second variable leads the observer to make legitimacy the key dynamic that controls this capacity 2.

Figure 4.4 characterizes capacity 2 and its horizontal axis of the dynamic of legitimacy for regulation. Indeed, the full exercise of this capacity to propose change and the technical regime that makes it possible is subject to the major problem of the legitimacy of its content. The territory, therefore, can be perceived based on this dynamic as the place of competition among solutions argued to regulate. Territories can thus be in very different situations as to the legitimacy of the technical regimes they employ.

Figure 4-4: The dynamic capacity of the territorial development

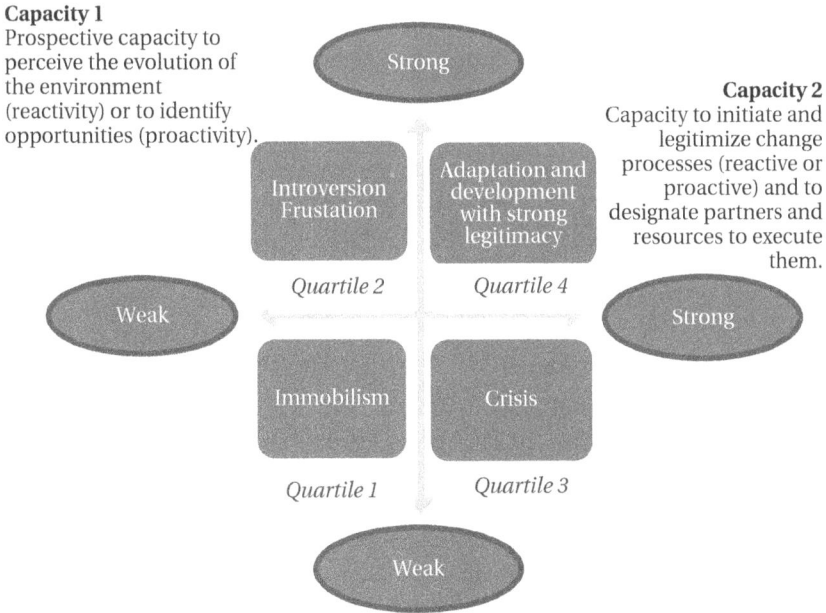

Capacity 1
Prospective capacity to perceive the evolution of the environment (reactivity) or to identify opportunities (proactivity).

Capacity 2
Capacity to initiate and legitimize change processes (reactive or proactive) and to designate partners and resources to execute them.

Strong

Introversion Frustation

Adaptation and development with strong legitimacy

Quartile 2

Quartile 4

Weak

Strong

Immobilism

Crisis

Quartile 1

Quartile 3

Weak

Figure 4.4 makes comparison on the axis of capacity 2, the territorial situations in which no regulation imposes itself as chiefly legitimate (weak). In this case, the ability to regulate (weak) is subject to competition among the stakeholders dominated by the uncertainty of divergent opinions or by the lack of competition resulting from the deficiency of divergent opinions or the omnipresence of routines or tradition. This (weak) capacity is opposed to a (strong) capacity that the possible debate on the technical regime has been concluded in favor of an option in terms of the potential combination of partners and resources. To refine the dynamic capacity of a territory, capacity 1 contrasts with a weak capacity for governance, for perceiving changes in the environment or for identifying opportunities with a strong capacity to involve many parties, namely stakeholders in its vision of the future.

The crossover of these two variables in Figure 4.4 reveals four quartiles. They seek to synthesize some issues of territorial development according to the TVF. Figure 4.4 allows the analyst to retain the main and approaching features of the situation of each territory from the specific association of its existing dynamics.

Quartile 1 –Immobilism- This quartile highlights the major features of a territory that presents difficulties in fixing prospects given the state of its environment and the truncated opportunities considered by the stakeholders. It combines this weakness with many difficulties in proposing avenues for changes or considering new ones. In this quartile, the dynamic of decision or governance, dominated by the Top-down, have chronically used the same relational functions that leave little room for emerging initiatives or rarely include stakeholders who do not have power and whose legitimacy is struggling to gain recognition.

The dynamic of alert is often unable, given the prospects, to formulate priorities and risks disappearing out of resignation. This bleak picture describes development prospects that can only come from outside in the context of a policy of aid or economic rebalancing or in that of projects for new activities capable of creating resilience and rebirth of dynamics and relational functions. In less severe forms, the analysts can find indicators of immobility in the strong domination of the dynamics of decision and governance whose relational functions are limited and have not evolved over a long period.

Quartile 2 -Introversion-Frustration- This quartile describes a paradoxical territorial situation. In this quartile, the stakeholders who hold power and are the "prime resources integrators" in the dynamics of decision-making and governance often clearly define their medium-term ambitions for the territory. From experience, they know all the opportunities that they think available to the territory. These ambitions are often linked to the territory's historical capacity to exploit a specific resource or knowledge. The high level of conception of the future is, in their eyes, obvious and leaves little room for controversy. The stakeholders involved in decision-making and governance, as well as expertise and communication, often have direct interests in the exploitation of this resource and have intensely captured all the dynamic of legitimacy over the long term. The paradox of this situation is that this enormous awareness of the future of the territory leads the main dynamics relational functions to be highly selective. They easily exclude legitimacy of all messages coming from the dynamics of opposition, alert, or even expertise not recognized by the government. The obviousness of the territory's "mission", as it saturates the dynamics of legitimacy, marginalizes the propositions that challenge the existing technical and normative regime as self-evident. It also challenges plans to diversify activities presented as a possible weakening of the effectiveness of guidance.

The power and fight for legitimacy are at the heart of the definition of this quartile. The legitimacy (weak in Figure 4.4) appears rather as the result of a balance of power. When power and legitimacy realize the difficulties of leaving room for other stakeholders and when a few relational functions are established for sharing, in spite of the relativity, this state of exclusion creates introversion and frustration for all those who believe that they are carriers of transition (such as economic, environmental or cultural transition) and are not heard.

Quartile 3 -Crisis- This quartile analyzes several key features of the territory in crisis. The TVF observes this crisis as a struggle among divergent opinions on the directions to be adopted. This struggle is more critical since it affects the dynamics of governance and decision. Without any imposed guidelines (weak in Figure 4.4), this struggle is further exacerbated by the dynamic of legitimacy that pushes the different actors to develop the details of the technical and normative regime of their own orientations, to try and to succeed.

In this particularly volatile quartile, a large number of development dynamics enter into crisis. The relational functions established in each dynamic are reconfigured, with an attempt to break the deadlock into which the development dynamic of the territory is plunged. In this situation, the dynamics of decision and governance can disappear for a moment in favor of the dynamics that do not have power but try to possess one, allowing all these concerned stakeholders the opportunity to be heard.

Quartile 4 -Adaptation and development with strong legitimacy- This quartile updates and bring the elements collectively in order to create a general and sustainable dynamic of territorial development. They reveal the importance of a permanent reflection on the future and the opportunities of the territory. The quartile favors the fact that a high level of reflection and conception is associated with a high level of legitimacy in development. The MLP, by activating the question on the orientations and on "what to do?" and "with whom to do it?", consequently leads to reaching these two high levels thanks to deliberative and collaborative governance.

Governance is based on the recognition of the Bottom-up that integrates stakeholders who only have power through this recognition. Such governance is exercised without the prerogatives of sited, because Top-Down is contradicted to maintain an acceptable level of tension between understanding (relevance of the interpretation of opportunities) and extension (legitimacy).

Similarly, the SPT places the question on "how to do it?" and "in which type of resource combination and from whom?". The search for the technical and normative regime is an opportunity to develop the relational functions of all development dynamics. These functions become the means to widen the circle of actors. The analysts, based on these indicators alone, can find, in the TVF points of support to characterize, the general state of a territorial dynamic of development.

It is clear that these four quartiles offer only a sketch of a general diagnosis of territory development. A concrete analysis of territory will certainly often lead to the observation that is a mixed form of these quartiles that best describes the pursued trend. The analysts may be interested particularly in the presence of a given territory of each mentioned dynamic and their relational functions. Each quartile shows a specific configuration of these two objects, and the dynamic of territorial development is widely explained by the variations of this configuration.

To take stock of a particular development situation, two sets of questions sum up the process. The first set is: where does the territory lie, in the broadest possible integration of the dynamics and relationships they generate among stakeholders to promote development prospects? The second one is: who are the stakeholders and in which relational functions do they achieve proven mastery of the most effective technical and normative regimes? And how do they ensure the legitimacy of their solutions to make the territorial offers as attractive as possible?

The next chapter, Chapter 5, is devoted to the third tool, the "Cube Service Value" or the "CSV" for policymakers. This tool aims to strengthen the quality of the technical regime for territorial propositions. It gives some rules that are likely to make these propositions as attractive as possible for the beneficiaries and thus promote territorial development by strengthening the influence of its contents.

Bibliography

Clarkson, M. 1994. "A risk based model of stakeholder theory." *Proceedings of the Second Toronto Conference on Stakeholder Theory*, Toronto: Center for corporate social performance and Ethics, University of Toronto.

Freeman, R.E. 1984. *Strategic Management: A Stakeholder approach.* Boston: Pilman.

Freeman, R.E. and Reed, D.L. 1983. "Stockholders and stakeholders: A new perspective on corporate governance." *California Management Review* 25, 3: pp. 93-94.

Freeman, R.E. Harrison, J.S. Wicks, A.C. Parmar, B.L. and De Colle, S. 2010. *Stakeholder Theory, The State of the Art.* Cambridge University Press.

Hill, C.W.L. Jones, T.M. 1992. "Stakeholders-agency theory." *Journal of Management Studies* 29, 2: pp. 131-154.

Mitchell, R.K, Agle, B.R, Wood, D.J. 1997. "Toward a theory of stakeholder identification and salience: Defining the principle of who and what really counts." *Academy of Management Review* 22, 4: pp. 853-886.

Moeller, S. 2010. "Characteristics of services –a new approach uncovers their value." *Journal of Services Marketing* 24, 5: pp. 359-368.

Pallemaerts, M. Moreau, M. 2004. *The role of stakeholders in international governance of environment.* (November) Paris: IDDRI.

Vargo, S.L. 2008. "Customer integration and value creation: paradigmatic traps and perspectives." *Journal of Service Research* 11, 2: pp. 211-215.

Vargo, S.L. and Lusch, R.F. 2004. "Evolving a New Service Dominant Logic for Marketing." *Journal of Marketing* 68 (January): pp. 1-17.

Wicks, A.C. Gilbert, D.D.jr. Freeman, R.E. 1994. "A feminist reinterpretation of the stakeholder concept." *Business Ethics Quarterly* 4, 4: pp. 475-497.

Chapter 5

Method and Tool 3:
The Cube Service Value (CSV)

5.1 Tool 3: the Cube Service Value (CSV)

The territorial action plan seeks to give the providers the means of governance and regulation to optimize the implementation of the actions and their expected results.

The question of better effectiveness of service propositions (the bulk of territorial offers), of their efficiency and their ability to innovate and to create increasing value is, therefore, frequently asked. These questions attempt to find an answer from the components of service satisfaction for the beneficiary. Two components of this satisfaction are generally gaining attention (Mayer et al. 2003): a structural and situational component. The first, purely technical, touches, on the different stages, the resources and the tasks of the service offer (Booms and Bitner 1981, Shostack 1992). The second, purely situational, includes all the interactions experienced by the producer/beneficiary couple during the same service provision (Grönross 1984), as well as the perceptions committed by the beneficiary in the experience of the service provision. Both fuel judgments of satisfaction or dissatisfaction.

For designing and facilitating territorial policies, the tool proposed here, under the term Cube Service Value (CSV) (Felix and Garcia 2017) (Felix, Ben Mimmoun and Garcia 2021) aims to improve quality and innovation in the territorial service offer. It encompasses both governance, proposing a suitable collaboration among stakeholders, and regulation, identifying the sensitive points of territorial offers that can be improved or redesigned by innovative proposals. As part of the TVF, the CSV proposes key questions about a territorial offer as well as a method to deal with them.

The CSV pinpoints the sensitive elements of any territorial service offer to propose improvement or innovation strategies for each of them. It gives access to service improvements or innovations (incremental or disruptive innovations).

The CSV conceptual framework is constructed on two references: the properties of the IHIP service and the time, more particularly, the stages of service provision and the beneficiary's path of the service offer. These steps define a before-, a during- and an after- provision, closely associated with the values contained in the service proposition and, more specifically, the so-called "potential values, values in exchange and values in use" that the cube links according to Chapter 2.

Applied to territorial offers, the crossing of the IHIP properties and time-values take the dimensions of a cube by adding the third dimension: the seven elements of the mix-service (7P)[1]. These elements are available to service producers to design and concretely implement their offers. These 7Ps summarize all the means of expressing the offer and ensuring its attractiveness. These means extend from the characteristics of the service, its pricing, its communication and its distribution, through the behavior of the agents in contact and their procedures, to the material or immaterial means that accompany the information, the service and the service monitoring.

In the use of CSV, this third dimension can only be exploited effectively if the stakeholders producing the service enter into the details of these 7 dimensions. They can then be the subject of an assessment of the current offer and of a search for improvement or even innovation on the twelve sensitive points proposed by the CSV.

In this book, this detailed work for the multiple offers of the cultural theme of the three territories studied could not be carried out. Given the impossibility of bringing together all the interlocutors directly involved in the process for the three territories, this part of the CSV could not be the subject of information gathering. However, the contribution of this third dimension of 7Ps is a step in the development of the complete TVF method.

5.2 Time structuring of territorial offers

The CSV retains two structural dimensions of time:

The first deals with the treatment of before-, during- and after- provision. It usually refers to the notion of customer's path or blueprinting (Bitner et al. 2008). The CSV pays particular attention to the after-provision that the blueprint approach does not take into account focusing rather on operational efficiency until the end of the service provision.

The second touches on the duration of the service.

The CSV places emphasis specifically on the issue of the duration of resource transformation. On the observation as seen in Chapter 2, the interface can only

[1] The seven classical mix elements known as the 7Ps are Product, Price, Promotion, Place, Physical evidence, People, and Process. All these concepts are introduced in later subsections.

be a prerequisite with sacrifices to obtain after the benefits of use. The CSV encourages the evaluation of the service duration as a structural feature. It searches for improvements or innovations capable of reducing this duration, by augmented reality, real-time control, connected and geolocated objects, priority access ticket online, etc., lengthening the duration like augmented reality, connected objects, personalization, goods free of complementary services, "opportunities for wonder", and other surprises, or even watering it down by introducing desirable dimensions in a "sacrificial" scenario.

By taking the time in its structural form, the CSV gives itself the means to reinforce the attractiveness of the offer. It integrates the contents of the beneficiary's experience as strategic objects according to the before-, during- or after- service. It offers an opening that complements the only issues of blueprinting and episodes of contact between producer and beneficiary.

5.2.1 Values in territorial offers

The issue of values co-production and co-creation through the joint action of service producers and beneficiaries has been driving for more than a decade (Vargo and Lusch 2004a, 2004b). The CSV, according to the developments of Chapter 2 and the "Facilities-Transformation-Use" (FTU) approach (Moeller 2008), associates the definition of the values in offer proposition with the temporal progress of the service provision.

Before the provision, the resources of the producer help the beneficiary to imagine the chances of a successful transformation followed by desired uses, if the producers communicate via physical persons, productive and intermediate goods, skills and knowledge, data, nominal goods, and so on. Moreover, if the producers strategically invest this before, they can endow their resources with potential value.

During the service provision, the producer of the territorial offer tries to solve the beneficiary's problems by making them his own and integrates the customers' requirements into his value chain (Kleinaltenkamp et al. 1997). Problems related to the nature of the beneficiary's resources, those that may arise during the combination and transformation of these resources, lead the producers to improve or innovate in all forms of co-production, namely the specific sources of values in exchange development.

The end of the service provision marks the end of the beneficiaries' resources transformation. An after-service provision begins for them, manifesting the desired uses. The literature is in debate since the appearance of the Service Dominant Logic (SDL) (Vargo and Lusch 2004a, 2006). The CSV attempts to characterize whether this value in use is always an "interactive" creation, a co-creation between the producers and the beneficiaries. It is particularly interested in the type of interaction that needs to be maintained between the producers and the beneficiaries in or outside the after-service provision, to make them creators or co-creators of values in use.

The CSV formalizes the opportunity for the producers to maintain the interactions with his beneficiaries, influencing the emergence of new values in use in an interactive and joint process of co-creation or in a process of facilitation, creation or even transfer or capture of value (Cova and Dalli 2009).

Thus, strategic thinking on territorial offers structures itself by crossing the properties of services (the IHIP) with time and the values associated with them.

The aim of the CSV is to bring out as many managerial issues through this cross that can guide improvement or innovation projects. Each scenario resulting from this cross provides the opportunity to identify and deal with a large number of concrete situations, all called for by the practical responses they elicit in playing their roles in the competitive positioning of the service to be managed.

5.2.2 The characteristics of territorial service offers according to time and values

The CSV firstly proposes to cross, in a double-entry table, the main characteristics of the territorial service offers with the time and the values that help to structure and guide the governance and regulation of action plans.

Table 5-1: CSV Cross tabulation

IHIP	Definition	Potential Values (Before-provision)	Values in use (After-provision)	Values in exchange (During-provision)
Intangibility 1	Difficulties for beneficiaries to form a mental picture of the service and its effects	1A	1B	1C
Heterogeneity 2	Difficulties of the service provider and the beneficiary to give constantly the same resources to combine.	2A	2B	2C
Inseparability 3	Difficulties to optimize the provider-beneficiary encounter by extending or reducing the encounter duration	3A	3B	3C
Perishability 4	Difficulties to support and extend the reality of the offer when the uses are over and difficulties to develop loyalty	4A	4B	4C

From this cross-tabulation, 12 sensitive points of the territorial offers are defined for strategic thinking and action. The first line of the table is devoted to the treatment of intangibility in service offers. This treatment is particularly justified because it creates uncertainty for the beneficiaries, difficulty in discriminating and choosing between several offers, and leads to an increased perception of risks (Rushton and Carson 1989, Laroche et al. 2003).

Line 1: line of entries in the territorial offer and help for beneficiaries to form a mental picture of the service facilities, the interface, and the uses.

Table 5-2: Intangibility

Time - Values	Potential Values (Before- provision)	Values in exchange (During- provision)	Values in use (After- provision)
Intangibility 1	Reduce the perceived risks of beneficiaries by communicating information on the *search qualities* of the offer proposition, by giving the beneficiaries enough to represent all the facilities and resources made available to them if the offer proposal is accepted.	Reduce the perceived risks of beneficiaries by communicating information on the *experiential qualities* of the offer proposition, by giving the beneficiaries enough to represent the co-production path and all what happens within the service provision and what kind of resources are required to be combined.	Reduce the perceived risks of beneficiaries by communicating information on the *credence qualities* of the offer proposition, by giving the beneficiaries enough to represent all the benefits of the uses to be expected from the offer once the service is rendered.
	1 A	1 B	1 C

Square 1A:

For the producers, the treatment of intangibility focuses, firstly, on the search qualities (Zeithaml 1981) that is likely to provide the beneficiaries with attractive mental pictures encouraging the acceptance of the proposed service offer. The attention paid to the expression of these search qualities concerns merely as much the prospect to be transformed for the first time, as the experienced beneficiaries who may be looking for a strong re-anchoring of the impressions left by experience fostering a new acceptance of the service offer.

These search qualities are to be found in all the resources that the producers can make available to the beneficiaries. In this sense, the treatment of intangibility results in potential value propositions reinforcing the attractiveness of the service, while the decision to accept and engage in the service provision has not been made yet. Literature (Levitt 1981, Berry and Clark 1986, Mittal 2002) offers before-acceptance of the service several physical tangibility techniques applied to these search qualities. These techniques affect, in particular, the physical environment of the service called the "serviscape" (Lovelock et al. 2004). All of these techniques aim to reinforce the materiality of the service in the beneficiary's mind. Berry and Clarke (1986) suggest four types of techniques for making a service offer tangible through communication. The first one is the visualization favoring high-value imagery factors such as brands, logos, characters, symbols, etc., reinforced by digital applications. The second and third ones are the associations that give the imagery factors like logos, characters; or verbal like slogans). The last type of technique is a valence capable of arousing positive mental images related to the service (Felix and Sempels 2009), for example, in open days, restaurants opening a common space with their kitchen. Virtual visits in augmented reality or visual mental imagery factors serve as the lifeline to characterize an IT assistance service. This square must use physical or virtual channels to provide the beneficiaries with good mental representations of the key characteristics of the service used for the offer examination or the updating of experience expressing potential values, as many points of support for an acceptance decision.

Square 1B:

This square characterizes a very little studied strategic situation in terms of reducing intangibility in services. Before purchase, making incentive the service implies two different forms of intangibility that are not limited to the difficulties of perceiving the search qualities through the senses. Square 1B introduces the intangibility of generality and mental intangibility as essential forms of intangibility to be reduced when the client seeks to have a good mental picture of how the proposed interface will work (Dubé-Rioux et al. 1990). This form of intangibility essentially affects the experiential qualities of service. It anticipates when the interface occurs and transforms the beneficiaries' resources. Mental intangibility refers to the difficulty for a service to be understood and summarized mentally in its functioning and its effects (like legal services, banking, insurance, real estate, medical care, and so on). As Lovelock and Gummesson (2004) note, the mental intangibility of a service does not necessarily depend on its physical intangibility. It can be determined by the judgment of the service producers on what are the experiential qualities that it is advisable to provide strong representations and how much it is desirable to express them to reach the degree of specificity (reduction of generality) and the mental construction of the beneficiary's path. The stimulation of these representations ensures the positioning of the service offer. In such a context, Square 1B has the strategic objective of measuring all the promises of values in exchange that accompany the service interface and the co-production of the transformation contained in this promise. This square is the place to reflect on all the co-production facilities likely to strengthen the offer proposition. Examples are from mechanical parts changed on a vehicle, providing clients with so many experiential qualities and "DIY" sheets, the following up of the customer's work by Webcam, avatars guiding through the interface scenarios, to the geolocation of the operations in progress or the accesses available to the service.

Square 1C:

It addresses mainly the credence qualities of the service. Before the service, it makes the service be able to bring about mental representations of its usage values a vital strategic element of its attractiveness. Laroche et al. (2001) show that the intangibility created by the beneficiary's difficulty in evaluating performance and the service benefits is often independent of the physical tangibility of this service, especially when the beneficiary lacks experience or needs reinsurance.

The guarantees thus run out if the management of the service does not offer support for the mental picture of the uses and specific advantages to be expected from the service. From classic testimonials of the "before" and "after" type, passing through authorized labeling or simulations are examples of reassurance.

The second line of the CSV addresses the service and its potentials for innovations and quality improvements from the second key dimension of any service provision: heterogeneity.

Line 2: The line of provider-client co-production, taking into account the resources involved in the exchange and in promoting the variety of uses.

More specifically here, the CSV emphasizes the beneficiary's resources. As a whole, the literature on service heterogeneity points out the difficulty of its standardization (Edgett and Parkinson 1993). This approach focuses the thinking on improving procedures by reducing individual differences among providers (such as staff training, uniforms, rules for welcoming and contacting customers and providing all forms of automation).

Table 5-3: Heterogeneity

Time - Values	Potential Values (Before provision)	Values in exchange (During provision)	Values in use (After provision)
Heterogeneity 2	Show supply-side consideration of cases where heterogeneity of producer-beneficiaries' resources can impede offer attractiveness and reduce perceived risk to beneficiaries of difficulties in providing expected resources	Propose appropriate co-production paths based on the expressed recognition of heterogeneity of resources that beneficiaries must provide and combine. Show that producers take all measures to facilitate exchanges in co-production	Make the offer attractive and value it by showing how all the beneficiaries get the same benefits from the uses or how each of them, whatever their resources and their ability to combine them, finds adapted benefits
	2 A	2 B	2 C

It is supplemented by the question of resources that the beneficiary comes to combine and transform during the service encounter. The CSV, therefore, pays particular attention to identify the resources that the targeted beneficiaries are, in effect, capable of engaging in the service encounter.

These resources are described (Flieβ and Kleinaltenkamp 2004) in Chapter 2, such as physical resources (the client himself), possessions, rights, nominal assets or personal data as well as skills or modes of representation or affect, degrees of disposition or implication, and time availability (Palmer and Cole 1995).

Square 2A:

It concentrates the strategic thinking on the resources that the service offer has to mobilize so that the promise of use is fully kept regardless of the individual differences in providers, time of delivery and context. The nature of the co-production in the transformation of the client's resources makes it possible to note a low or high heterogeneity of its available resources. Becoming a client of a real estate crowdfunding or fast food service does not require the same commitment of resources. This never-naive question, even when it comes to choosing a signage system for a parking service, looms the key question of the physical and psychological accessibility of the transformation contained in the promise of service and, therefore, in the "serviscape" (Lovelock et al. 2004) described as the set of physical and symbolic elements contributing to making a service accessible. The CSV's reference to the notion of literacy (Chrisomalis 2009)[2] and the beneficiary's ability to encode and decode information or to build meanings from a given medium in a given technical (digital) social or cultural context is at stake here.

Square 2B:

It raises the question of adapting encounter modes to the resources available to customers. This adaptation of the resource combination has budgetary implications that can be serious. They are to be arbitrated according to the new accessibility and value creation they allow. Creating a "child" or "visually impaired" route in a museum, offering receptions and treatment methods for cars departing from airports for business classes, walk-in services, the provision of tools, and advice for those who want to make their own mechanical repairs, all these adaptations are based on a finding of customer resources heterogeneity that service producers can choose to offer. For instance, when the development of a real estate finance service realizes that its customers are essentially professional investors initiated into the intricacies of real estate finance, it becomes a significant strategic moment and objective of attracting small savers who can access property by buying shares to meet the heterogeneity of the target resources. This square naturally feeds Square 1B on the tangibility of the proposed co-production route(s).

Square 2C:

This square seeks to develop two possible strategies in innovative solutions, either to enhance the consideration by service producers of the multiplicity of uses and the benefits they make possible or to emphasize that the offer takes care to deliver the same promises of uses and benefits regardless of the differences in resources provided by the beneficiaries. The possible strategies refer to "late adaptations" through "all-inclusive" and "selling results" in the economy of service functionality[3]. It extends to all forms of recognition of specific uses linked to all digital or non-pre-registration solutions (database, concierge services, digital recognition, etc.). The implementation of these solutions can fuel Squares 2A and 2B and even Squares 1B and 1C, insofar as they contribute to reinforce the potential values of the offer by closely conforming to the beneficiary (2A) or they express values in exchange

---

[2] Literacy is defined as a capability to read and interpret the meaning of a system of signs (verbal, scriptural, symbolic, etc.)

[3] The selling results are based on the sale of performance of use and not on the simple sale of goods.

contained in a service corresponding to the level of resources that the client is ready to commit (1B and 1C). It proposes a choice of real paths (2B) or a range of values in use delivered by the offer (2C).

Line 3: The line of the development of service encounters and the production of experience, sources of satisfaction for beneficiaries

The CSV places particular emphasis on the duration of the service and co-production for the benefit of customer satisfaction. The duration of the service appears as an opportunity to strengthen the control of the service and its impact on satisfaction. Duration is the very structure of the service lending itself to improvements and innovations. The waiting time often dominant in the analysis of the duration of the service is analyzed in the CSV as a simple situational dysfunction.

Table 5-4: Inseparability

Time - Values	Potential Values (Before provision)	Values in exchange (During provision)	Values in use (After provision)
Inseparability 3	Diagnosis of the coproduction encounter in terms of pleasure or displeasure, possibilities for the beneficiary of positive experiences, the association of values in exchange and values in use during the encounter	Strategic choices to extend or reduce encounters duration according to whether they are sources of pleasure or displeasure and reinforce the values in exchange during these encounters by the first provision of values in use	Strategic choices to develop customer "performance" to benefit as many values in use as possible by suggestions and evocations regarding uses, and maintain opportunities to produce favorable experience by new encounters
	3 A	**3 B**	**3 C**

Square 3A:

The diagnosis divides the "during" of the service into main sequences: necessary duration of the tasks to be accomplished, foreseeable duration of the transformation of the beneficiary's resources, and the waiting period of the client (Stuart and Tax 1997). This breakdown mainly relates to the interface, but can also relate to the periods of entry and exit of this interface. This "blueprinting" is associated in this box with a set of evaluation: are the interface sequences created by the service producer a source of pleasant or unpleasant experience for the customer? How and how far to extend a sequence when it seems pleasant? How to reduce its duration if it is considered unpleasant?

Likewise, does the service encounter produce values in exchange that have already contained values in use? This is particularly the case when consumption begins with the combination of resources, considering the case in which the physical resource to be combined is the beneficiary himself (transport, body care, leisure, education, etc.) (Moeller 2008). The square also poses another important question: are the promised values in use already experimented at the time of the encounter? If this is not the case, for instance, there are incidents or matters like having medical treatment, visiting a dentist, obtaining a registration card or a residence permit and so on, are these values in use obtained despite the deemed unpleasant nature of the encounter and offset by the promise of value in use justifying some interface displeasure? This strategic question reflects on the "willing to pay" or the beneficiary's satisfaction (Mizik and Jacobson 2003), and on all the measures to be taken presented above (such as the mitigation of the client's apprehensions linked to intangibility, recognition and assumption by the producer of all the heterogeneity factors that could be dissuasive under the known formula of "this offer is not for me"). In this square, the CSV puts the values in exchange at the heart of the system to be built. Associated by nature with the co-production encounter, they must mobilize all the resources of the producer to provide the beneficiary with a clear vision of everything done for him to increase his pleasures or reduce his displeasure during the transformation period.

All these resources should lead to a customer experience where the values in exchange are always enriched with more values in use, and, if that is impossible, to an experience where values in exchange always encourage beneficiaries to accept "sacrificial" encounters to obtain deferred values in use made more accessible or desirable like those of common goods or intergenerational transmissions.

Square 3B:

It organizes the implementation of values in exchange in the encounters by focusing them on two issues related to customer's experience. They are the issue of duration to be reduced or extended according to pleasure or displeasure to expect from the encounter, and the issue of added value reinforcement for producers and the satisfaction for beneficiaries when it is possible to enhance the values in exchange with values in use and to reduce interfaces deemed unpleasant. This is the objective sought by mobile solutions for car repairs or troubleshooting of agricultural machines by helicopter allowing the failed harvester to avoid penalties for delay in the delivery of his crop to the cannery. In addition, the extension and enrichment of encounters are observable in the evolution of banking points of sales inspired by "Web live shopping", including "surprise" spaces or in 24-hour Web-assistance or as in DIY activities or in promotional campaigns of hairdressing brands offering free massages, and so on. Conversely, we are witnessing the attempt to reduce the encounter time in applications dedicated to the reservation of various services or in monitoring the logistical progress of delivery or in making no queue tickets available. This square concretizes all improvements and innovations acquired in the strategic control of the interface. It ranges from extension or reduction of the encounter duration to the enrichment of service experience in all its dimensions (educational, cultural, playful or social), of emotional discovery and of incentive to participate (Rodie and Kleine 2000, Teixeira et al. 2012),

Square 3C:

This square is that of the exploitation of the possible coexistence between values in exchange and values in use. If the values in use are deemed to intervene when the interface and the transformation that it allows are finished, revealing uses from the moment of the combination appears as a powerful lever of influence on the acceptance of the service.

When it fails to combine values in exchange and values in use, the Square 3C must establish how to benefit from as many values in use as possible at the end of the transformation. Some of which may be new and optional, to be created or co-created at the choice of the beneficiaries. Square 3C is thus the square for suggestions and evocations of possible uses. It is also that of the development of learning, socialization or enhancement interfaces that open a "constellations of uses" (Vargo 2008) for the beneficiaries, once the service has been rendered and during which the service producer can play the role of co-creator or simple "facilitator" of values in use (Caru and Cova 2015). There are abundant examples of possible sources improving or innovating the performance of the beneficiary (Bateson 2002), ranging from the pooling of experiences, social network issues bringing communities of users together, the newsletters on the service news, including user testimonials or the exchange of computerized data on the availability of an offer, to the use of an offer and the access it gives to the uses of other offers.

Line 4: The loyalty line and tools for renewing uses and co-creating new values in use.

The CSV exploits the perishability of the service as a possible source of improvement and innovation. The perishability of the service reveals the direct dependence of the offer on the beneficiary's resources. An online reservation center, an application to manage appointments, yield management or pricing policy and free access to a show provided beneficiary confirm his attendance by email, all these means come to the aid of perishability when it essentially applies to people rather than to objects or data from the beneficiary. On this line, the CSV places particular emphasis on the managerial problem linked to after-service: the conservation and the renewal and extension of values in use to build customer loyalty.

Table 5-5: Perishability

Time - Values	Potential Values (Before provision)	Values in exchange (During provision)	Values in use (After provision)
Perishability 4	Raise the customer's favorable judgment on all the values in use offered by the offer. Build territorial information and monitoring systems to identify positive externalities of uses resulting from the service provision, sources of possible loyalty by co-creation or even facilitation, transfer or capture of values in use	In collaboration with the beneficiaries, develop values in exchange through the call to expertise or citizen mediation by digital means or not on the evolution of uses or new uses, to promote them as renewals or extensions of service promises by co-creation, facilitation, transfer or capture of values in use	Open spaces for co-creation, facilitation, transfer or capture of values in use to observe positive externalities. Develop the struggle against perishability of the offer through creating new service encounters to exploit these positive externalities as renewal or extension of service promised values
	4 A	4 B	4 C

Square 4A:

This square is at the heart of a strategic reflection on the nature of the service effects from the point of view of uses, on the forms of keeping them in the customer's mind and, especially, on the forms of their extension or renewal. When the perishability of the service has done its work, so, building customer's loyalty becomes strategic

To deal directly with this issue, the CSV must use three key concepts: the effects or benefits from which the client derives its appreciation of their values in use, the salience or the "memorabilia" of these values once the uses have perished, and the externalities of these uses. These externalities should be comprehended as the unforeseen and unsolicited effects of the transformation, capable of extending uses by new uses and of extending their value.

The CSV attempts to present a conceptual device that enables practitioners to find their landmarks in the vast debate on producer-beneficiary co-creation of values in use. It essentially seeks to delimit strategically what is co-production and what is co-creation of these values. According to the CSV, the notion of externality offers such an opportunity.

These externalities can be sources of co-creation for the producer if he can build the information systems that maintain his strength of value proposition. These positive externalities can also be sources of transfer or capture of values in use if the client creates unforeseen uses from these externalities. Thus, social services, leisure or educational monitoring organizations, and territorial or commercial agents in the field know that observing what the beneficiaries do with the services or goods offered to them constitutes an important source of innovation and renewal of offers.

This square is also interested in the perpetuation in the beneficiary's mind of the relationship between the service and the values in use that it offers to counter its perishability (Tversky and Kahneman 1974). It suggests an interesting perspective to guide loyalty actions. This heuristic is close to the attribution judgment and the persistence of this judgment. The service producer is invited with the beneficiary to arouse a favorable judgment on all of the values proposed by his offer and, in particular, the values in use, and to fuel this first inference by a strategy of dissemination of information ensuring its adjustment, serving as a confirmation of the anchoring, and, consequently, its sustainability.

Square 4B:

This square focuses on the perspectives presented in Square 4A. Oriented on the values in exchange, these perspectives spur the service producer to center his information system on the values in exchange attached to his offer and on their effects on uses and their externalities. All forms of collaboration and information sharing with beneficiaries, all expertise and citizen mediation are pursued here. It is a question, in this case, of strengthening all the values in exchange based on the attention to the beneficiaries and the evolutions of their context of use. Thus, sufficient knowledge about the wishes of these beneficiaries, their attitudes and behaviors, for example, in terms of sports equipment leads a specialized distribution brand to extend the values in use offered to these customers by allowing them to recycle their equipment on second-hand markets. The flea market model reinforces brand-specific values in exchange[4].

Similarly, this square directly raises the question of the spontaneous creation of new values in use by the beneficiaries in identified externalities. New values that the service producer can transfer or capture in a strategy promote initiatives or support unexpected uses.

Square 4C:

It offers the operational perspectives to service strategists which enable them to manage all customer loyalty opportunities by extending values in use. In the presence of an information system that allows him to monitor the uses and assessments of these uses by the customer, the service producer can extend the promised values and, based on his strength of value proposition, becomes a co-creator or a simple facilitator of values in use according to their level of interaction with beneficiaries. Without the presence of a data collection system, the perishability of values in use is predictable unless the actions presented in Square 4B are launched. Monitoring the beneficiary's uses and the values that these externalities contain can fuel the expansion of uses.

It is possible, provided that the service producer knows how to seize all opportunities to know the value spontaneously created by customers. This is present in the unforeseen effects of the service experience and, more particularly, in the effects of the collective experience of this service. In the cultural field, a municipality, in a district of an old mining town, learns that neighbors spontaneously decide to collect postcards in their respective attics bringing the district mining history to life and to make it a private exhibition. The town hall facilitator of values in use simply proposes to run this exhibition as part of a twin-city program. In this sense, Square 4C encourages service producers to open observation spaces where, depending on the means and strategies available, they can develop facilitation, capture or co-creation of values of uses, loyalty and image building factors of the service producer.

This third CSV tool associated with that of the stakeholders can bring together in this chapter the essential benchmarks that condition the exercise of TVF. They alone give the keys necessary to develop a territorial action plan focused on immediate results driven by efficiency and creation of potentials from which the development of the territory can be envisaged and built.

---

[4] See Decathlon.fr

Bibliography

Bateson, J.E.G. 2002. "Consumer performance and quality in services." *Managing Service Quality* 12, 4: pp. 206-209.

Berry, L.L and Clark, T.1986. "Four ways to make services more tangible." *Business Horizons*: pp. 53-54.

Bitner, M. J. Ostrom, A. and Morgan, F.N. 2008. "Service Blueprinting: A Practical Technique for Service Innovation." *California Management Review* 50, 3 (Spring): pp. 66-94.

Booms, B. and Bitner, M.J. 1981. "Marketing Strategies and organization structures for service firms." In *Marketing of Services, American Marketing American Association*, edited by J Donnelly and W George. Chicago II.

Caru, A. and Cova, B. 2015. "Co-creating the collective service experience." *Journal of Service Management* 26, 2: pp. 276-294.

Chrisomalis, S. 2009. "The origins and co-evolution of literacy and numeracy" In *The Cambridge handbook of literacy*, edited by D.R Olson, N Torrance, 59-74. New-York: Cambridge University Press.

Cova, B. and Dalli, D. 2009. "Working consumers: the next step in marketing theory?" *Marketing Theory* 9, 3: pp. 315-339.

Dubé-Rioux, L. Regan, D.T. and Schmitt, B.H. 1990. "The cognitive representation of services varying in concreteness and specificity." *Advances in Consumer Research* 17: pp. 861-865.

Edgett, S and Parkinson, S. 1993. "Marketing for service industries". *The Services Industries Journal* 13, 3: pp. 19-39.

Felix, M. and Garcia, L. 2017. "CSV framework: a method to enrich service quality and innovation." *Working paper*, Skema Business School, Mercur lab (May): pp. 1-15.

Felix, M. and Sempels, C. 2009. "Service-Dominant Logic: Revisiting the Intangibility for a Sustainable Marketing." *the 2009 Naples Forum on Service, Service Dominant Logic, Service Science and Network Theory*, Capri (June): pp. 16–19.

Felix, M. Ben Mimmoun, S. and Garcia, L. 2021. "The Service Value Cube (SVC): How to make services theories fully usable for service managers" (in reviewing) *Journal of Service theory and practice.*

Flieβ, S. and Kleinaltenkamp, M. 2004. "Blueprinting the service company. Managing service processes efficiently." *Journal of Business Research* 57,4: pp. 392-404.

Grönross, C. 1984. "A service quality model and its marketing implications." *European Journal of Marketing* 18, 4: pp. 36-44.

Kleinaltenkamp, M. Ehret, M. and Flieβ, S. 1997. "Customer integration in Business to Business Marketing" In *Advances in Services Marketing*, edited by H Muhlbacher, J.P Flipo, 27-48. Wiesbaden, Germany: Gabler Verlag.

Laroche, M. Bergeron, J. and Goutaland, C. 2001. "A three-dimensional scale of the intangibility." *Journal of Service Research* 4, 1: pp. 26-38.

Laroche, M. Bergeron, J. and Goutaland, C. 2003. "How intangibility affects perceived risk: the moderating role of knowledge and involvement." *Journal of Services Marketing* 17, 2: pp. 122-140.

Levitt, T. 1981. "Marketing intangible products and product intangible." *Harvard Business Review* 59: pp. 94-102.

Lovelock, C. and Gummesson, E. 2004. "Wither Service Marketing? In Search of a new Paradigm and Fresh Perspective." *Journal of Service Research* 7, (August): pp. 20-41.

Lovelock, C. Wirtz, J. and Lapert, D. 2004. *Marketing des services,* Paris 5ième edition, Pearson Education France.

Mayer, K.J. Bowen, J.T. and Moulton, M.R. 2003. "A proposed model of the descriptors of service process." *Journal of Services Marketing* 17, 6: pp. 621-639.

Mittal, B. 2002. "Services Communications: from mindless tangibilisation to meaningful messages." *Journal of Services Marketing* 16, 5: pp. 421-431.

Mizik, N. and Jacobson, R. 2003. "Trading off between the Value Creation and Value Appropriation: The financial implications of shifts in Strategic Emphasis." *Journal of Marketing,* 67(January): pp.63-76.

Moeller, S. 2008. "Customer Integration- A key to an Implementation perspective of Service Provision." *Journal of Service Research* 11, 2: pp. 197-210.

Palmer, A. and Cole, C. 1995. *Service Marketing: Principles and Practice,* Englewood Cliffs, NJ: Prentice-Hall.

Rodie, A.R. and Kleine, S.S. 2000. "Customer participation in service production and delivery." In *Handbook of Services Marketing and Management,* edited by A.T Swartz and D Iacobucci, 111-125. Thousand Oaks, CA: Sage.

Rushton, A. and Carson, D.J. 1989. "The marketing of services: managing the intangibles." *European Journal of Marketing* 23, 8: pp. 23-44.

Shostack, G.L.1992. "Understanding services through blueprinting." In *Advances in Service Marketing and Management,* edited by A.T Swartz, D Bowen and S Brown, 1, Greenwich, CT JAI Press.

Stuart, F and Tax, S. 1997. "Designing and implementing new services: the challenge of integrating service." *Journal of retailing* 73, 1: pp. 105-134.

Teixeira, J. Patricio, L. Nunes, N. Nobrega, L. Fisk, R and Constantine, L. 2012. "Customer experience modelling: from customer experience to service design." *Journal of Service Management* 23, 3: pp. 362-373.

Tversky, A. and Kahneman, D. 1974. "Judgement under uncertainty: heuristics and biases" *Science* 185: pp. 1124-1131.

Vargo, S.L. 2008. "Customer integration and value creation: paradigmatic traps and perspectives." *Journal of Service Research* 11, 2: pp. 211-215.

Vargo, S.L. and Lusch, R.F. 2004a. "Evolving a New Service Dominant Logic for Marketing." *Journal of Marketing* 68 (January): pp. 1-17.

Vargo, S.L. and Lusch, R.F. 2004b. "The four service marketing myths: remnants of a goods-base manufacturing model." *Journal of Service Research* 6 (May): pp. 324-335.

Vargo, S.L. and Lusch, R.F. 2008. "Service-Dominant Logic: continuing the evolution." *Journal of the Academy of Marketing Science* 36, 1: pp. 1-10.

Zeithalm, L.V. 1981. *How Consumer Evaluation Processes Differ between Goods and Services.* Englewoods Cliffs, New York, Prentice Hall.

Chapter 6

How to Apply the TVF? A Six-Step Approach to Territorial Development

The application of the TVF to a territory uses a six-step analysis method. These six steps confront the concrete situation of territory with useful questions. According to the TVF, these steps gradually build up a synthetic evaluation of the possibilities for developing a territory and the actions to exploit them.

The aim of this chapter is, therefore, to set out this six-step method in depth. The book illustrates in the next chapter (chapter 7) these six steps with three examples of territories following the explanations of the methodological approach. This illustration compares, for each of these steps, three territorial development situations leading to three remarkably different analytical conclusions and specific action plans. These steps are as follows:

Table 6-1: Methodology steps

Methodology steps	The contents of the six steps of the TVF methodology
Step 1	Define the territory and its scope of intervention.
Step 2	Choose priority themes and their territorial development challenges.
Step 3	Identify the places and roles of stakeholders in each development theme. Select, among the seven development dynamics, those that are active for each theme.
Step 4	Diagnose, on each theme, the state of tension (understanding-extension) on the MLP axis. Observe the relational functions implied by the resources of the stakeholders and their combination in the offer propositions on the SPT axis.
Step 5	Conceive the most suitable forms of value creation for the offers of each thematic. Evaluate the technical and normative regime(s) ensuring the attractiveness of these propositions on the SPT axis using the CSV.
Step 6 To conclude this book	Evaluate the quality of the analysis (coherence, convergence and feasibility) and of the development plan, present in summary the innovations exploitable by the application of the TVF.

6.1 Define the territory

Step 1: Define the territory and its scope of intervention.

This first step aims to delimit the objects of the analysis: about what entity are we talking and what identification criteria should be used in order not to make territorial division errors and to bias the analysis? This step is obviously essential to the relevance of the overall analysis of the development challenges of the territory.

To be carried out correctly, this delimitation has to be multi-criteria. It has to respect the fact that territory is not limited solely to geographical borders. In this sense, the analysis should proceed by crosschecking to identify many usable criteria. Those will show the coherence of the object under the convergence of the criteria used.

In this work of the division, the geographical criteria (like physical or human) and the administrative criteria (such as regions, counties, departments, metropolises, communities of communes and so on according to the national organization) can serve as a starting point. When used alone, these criteria can occasionally blur development issues. So the criteria related to the political functions exercised on the territory endogenously (territorial functions) or exogenously with or without an adaptation system by delegated functions (territorialized function) can be added.

The criteria of political geography can be useful to include the division of the territory, the question of its degree of political and administrative autonomy. The answers to this question are valuable for identifying decisive or dominant stakeholders and for the strategic assessment of the territory by the MLP. In this context, the socio-cultural criteria that shape the collective representations of the actors' belonging to the territory can be crucial and helpful to delimit the territory and its "area of influence" or "marches". Many analyses relating to the territorial delimitation show the importance of the analysis of the actors' mobility and, in particular, that created by leisure transportations or by purchasing behaviors (marketable expenses).

In the views above, economic criteria are also beneficial, particularly those linked to exploitable physical or cultural resources, those that refer to the concepts of living or employment area or those that allow identifying local supplier-customer value chains or supply chains created or destroyed according to the history of the territory's activities. These criteria help to assess the evolution of the economic weight of the geographical entity over time. They, therefore, mark the evolution of a significant part of its influence.

In the first step, it is evident that analysts and policymakers must achieve a clear and distinct identification of the territory on the criteria subject to public judgment and capable of arousing the feeling of belonging for all the stakeholders to be affected. In this sense, this territorial delimitation leads to the key notion of "community of assumed interest", a real lever for societal involvement and development. The delimited territory is thus regarded as the relevant intervention territory.

6.2 Choose priority themes

Step 2: Choose priority themes and their territorial development challenges.

This second step defines the rules for the TVF analysis. To apply them, the TVF must select development paths on which the territory needs to focus its efforts as a priority. These tracks lead to themes integrating development actions, the strategic orientations they express, and the expected results. These themes specify the intervention area that should be broken down, at the operational level, into a series of different and complementary actions. Thus, general themes, such as tourism, culture, health, the renewal of the industrial or commercial fabric, and so on, find their expressions in various fields of action as many technical or normative regimes responsible for making them concrete.

The analysis of the development opportunities of the territory and its capacities to exploit them help to select the themes, to organize their modes of implementation, and to set their expected effects. These opportunities depend essentially on external factors that allow analyzing and predicting the evolution of the environment. They can be identified from classic approaches to strategic diagnosis (Weihrich 1982, Press 1990) as an incentive field [1] to cross with the strengths of the territory from an internal analysis. Lenz (1980), for example, identifies these strengths from three fundamental dimensions: the base of usable skills and technology in creating value, the ability to generate and acquire resources, and the managerial and administrative systems that can be mobilized. The method considers this step a strategic moment in the global analysis of the territory. The analyst is invited to interpret each of the selected themes from the angle of the opportunities of which he may or may not take advantage.

Likewise, the observable threats that represent obstacles to the development of each theme have to be identified. They are based on the same classic approach of diagnosis and presented as all the elements of the environment that risk affecting the territorial exploitation of opportunities. These threats are

---

[1] These incentives are essentially economic, technological, legal, social, cultural, demographic or political. See Stora 1974

to be crossed with the strengths and weaknesses of the territory. The questions of this strategic moment are then: "Are there existing development opportunities for the territory on the chosen theme?"; "Is the territory able to exploit these opportunities?"; "Are there threats to the exploitation of these opportunities?"; "Is the territory able to remove them?" and "Are the territory's policymakers able to translate these analyses into strategies?"

Among the important threats weighing on the development of a theme, the TVF retains a particular threat. It refers to the general dynamics of the development of a territory presented in Figure 4.4. The particular nature of this threat is that of a failure of the involved stakeholders to represent the evolutions of the environment and the offered opportunities (axis 1). Likewise, the threat lies in the second defect in representing and agreeing on the offer proposition and on the manner of implementing them (axis 2). This threat is present in three of the situations described in Figure 4.4: immobility, introspection-frustration and crisis. These situations condition the possibilities of exploiting the opportunities of each thematic. The analysis of the general dynamic of the development of a territory is, therefore, a prerequisite for any strategy of territorial development. This strategic moment should allow defining the set of measures to be taken to ward off this type of threat and relaunch the territory in a new development logic. To achieve this, it is necessary to perfectly satisfy the elements that characterize the situation of the territory in the quartile - adaptation and development with strong legitimacy.

This specific threat proposed by the TVF helps the territory to articulate clearly the external and internal dimensions of the diagnosis. It introduces the issues of the quality of the representations of the environment by stakeholders and that of the technical and normative regimes to be put in place for progress.

The diagnosis of the quality of these representations is a prerequisite for the analysis of all the threats that may weigh on the themes of territorial development. Its examination prepares the diagnosis of the third stage of the method devoted to the identification of stakeholders and the selection of development dynamics requested particularly by each of the selected themes.

This second step through Figure 4.4 assesses each thematic under the specific threat of difficulties in utilizing a general development dynamic. It thus seeks the key success factors for each theme. It prepares the reflection on the stakeholders in relation to power, legitimacy and urgency.

6.3 Identify the places and roles of stakeholders

Step 3: Identify the places and roles of stakeholders in each development theme. Select, among the seven development dynamics, those that are active for each theme.

The diagnosis of territorial development has to set up the places and roles of all the stakeholders involved in each thematic. The analysis should not only identify each stakeholder but characterize him according to the eight categories specified in Figure 4.2 and to their properties in Table 4.1.

The questions are: "To which category does a stakeholder belong?" and "What are the properties of this stakeholder?". It is then necessary to grasp the place and role of this stakeholder in the governance dynamic and to continue with the questions: "Do the relational factors of this governance dynamic show this stakeholder as a decision-maker or not?" and/or "What are the relational functions for non-decision-making stakeholders?" The questions posed here invite to start the analysis by the governance dynamic.

The answers to these questions guide an initial analysis of all the stakeholders, decision-makers or not, in the MLP governance axis, as presented in figure 3.2. Then, the analysis focus on the dynamics in which the involved stakeholders are the most engaged. Observers can draw a lot of information from the foregoing examination. This information is related to some dynamics that the theme involves, the relational functions that each dynamic maintains and with which category of stakeholders.

The analysis is carried out in two phases: one is a phase of identifying the stakeholders present in the design and implementation of the theme. This survey can be refined by selecting the stakeholders of each development dynamic concerned by this theme. The other phase is the functional analysis of identified stakeholders' roles. The analysis of the relational patterns among the identified stakeholders allows to observe exchanges in the different dynamics. According to the intensity of the exchanges and the number of stakeholders involved, the general dynamics of the theme appear. The multiplicity of the concerned stakeholders and the relational functions they maintain in the MLP and/or the SPT must be observed.

The main object for the observers is to qualify these relationships with reference to the governance dynamic and the decisive stakeholders. The relational functions of governance will offer an interesting perspective on the absence or atrophy of relationships. In this phase, the processes of communication, coordination, consultation, and even integration into the governance of non-decision-making stakeholders are directly perceptible for each theme.

It is possible to extend the analysis to the places and roles of the stakeholders who drive the opposition dynamic. The questions may be: "What are the categories of stakeholders who drive the opposition dynamic for this topic?" and/or "What treatment does the governance dynamic reserve for the dormant?" The question: "In this thematic, does the notion of non-public exist?" is often relevant. This question leads to another one: "Are the decision-making stakeholders capable of restoring the arguments of discretionaries or dependents?" At the end of this stage, the analysis of technological and, in particular, digital means (social networks, platforms, databases, dedicated sites, etc.) contributes to the evaluation of the places and roles of stakeholders in the theme.

6.4 Diagnose, on each theme, the state of tension

Step 4: Diagnose, on each theme, the state of tension (understanding-extension) on the MLP axis. Observe the relational functions implied by the resources of the stakeholders and their combination in the offer propositions on the SPT axis.

In the TVF, a central articulation distributes the places and roles of the stakeholders. It undoubtedly fixes their respective game depending on whether or not they participate in the relational functions on the MLP axis. It then leads to the examination of the relational functions engaged by these stakeholders to share resources and combine them in the value propositions of the technical and normative regime. These propositions constitute the offers on the SPT axis.

The continuation of the approach of this fourth step, therefore, consists in using the MLP/SPT articulation to better answer these questions: "How, in a territory, are the places and roles of stakeholders on development theme strengths or weaknesses for this theme?" and "In what way does the theme escape or undergo the threat of a general incapacity of the territory to conceive the orientations and the objectives or to agree on the technical and normative regime that will make the propositions for attractive offers?" Facing these questions, the analysts must firstly rule on the relational functions of governance, and then qualify the nature of the tensions that exist between emerging and sited partners by following figure 3.3.

It is required to examine both the methods of resolution of these tensions between understanding and extension and the treatment reserved for communication, concertation and the Bottom-Up cooperation as well as local or individual initiatives. From this perspective, the emergency dynamic is often useful for such an examination. It serves as a highly significant revealer of how the territory is able to resolve the tensions of the moment and for this purpose, to develop quickly its relational functions through communication, consultation and cooperation.

The key questions become: "What are the means and procedures used by the decisive stakeholders in governance to promote the emergence of individuals, ideas and innovations?"; "How do these stakeholders manage to give them a level of extension likely, by the way of example or model to follow, to reduce tensions between the individual and the general?" and "How are the decisive stakeholders able to practice forms of power-sharing or offer elaborate forms of consultation and co-production of decisions?"

The general objective of this fourth step is to set up the TVF, as presented in figure 3.2.

This reasoned implementation provides all the elements necessary to define the territorial policy that best corresponds to the territory analyzed according to tables 3.1, 3.2 and 3.3.

6.5 Conceive the most suitable forms of value creation

Step 5: Conceive the most suitable forms of value creation for the offers of each thematic. Evaluate the technical and normative regime(s) ensuring the attractiveness of these propositions on the SPT axis using the CSV.

This fifth stage directly deals, for each thematic, with the modes of value creation chosen by the territory. This value creation includes the composition of offer propositions in a technical and normative regime bringing together all the concerned stakeholders on the SPT axis. The analysis of this creation extends to the types of values that the offer proposition contains to give the desired attractiveness. The analysis, therefore, consists in identifying all the stakeholders who will be called upon to not only bring and combine their resources to produce value, but also to judge its attractiveness. The identification of these stakeholders, therefore, necessarily includes the stakeholders benefiting from the proposition. The definition of the territorial offer given in Chapter 2 underlines the participation of the beneficiary in the provision of resources and in their combination.

The questions are thus the following: "What are the specific offer propositions that contribute to the realization of the theme?"; "Are all the stakeholders who take part in the offer proposition completely identifiable?"; "What are the values that these stakeholders wish to deliver through their offer?"; "Do the statements of proposition objectives contain values other than use values?"; "Are the beneficiary stakeholders identified clearly?"; "Are these beneficiary stakeholders identified by segmentation by demand (a priori or a posteriori)[2] or do they fall under a segmentation by offer[3]?" and "Would the resources integration of other stakeholders be likely to enrich the value creation process?"

Identifying stakeholders and intentions to create value is the first part of this step. The second part of the analysis directly targets the contents of value creation and their contribution to the objectives of territorial development. After a phase of inventory bearing on the involved stakeholders and the nature of the combined resources, and, particularly, those of the beneficiaries, the examination relates to the offers' conception by the technical and normative regime and their capacity to exploit all the mechanisms of influence that will give theses offers all their attractiveness. In this second part of the fifth stage, it is the expertise of the technical and normative regime on the axis of the SPT that is evaluated in its capacity to conceive and express offer proposition strongly contributing to development. In such a context, given the definition of the offer proposition in Chapter 2, the service approach provides the basis for the analysis to be conducted.

Chapter 2 insists on the concept of co-production of the territorial offer. Such a concept conditions the expertise of the technical regime to its ability to develop the realization and attractiveness of offers by integrating beneficiary stakeholders. This integration, as shown in Chapter 2, concerns both participation in the production of the proposition and the actual value creation. To be carried out, this second part refers directly to the third tool called Cube Service Value (CSV) developed in the fifth chapter. The use of the CSV lends itself perfectly to a collective analysis of the stakeholders who produce each offer proposition (Felix, Ben Mimoun, Garcia 2021) and to answer, among others, the following questions: "What are the precise contents of the value propositions of the territorial offer?"; "How does the technical regulatory regime integrate the IHIP properties of territorial offers?"; "Does the territorial offer develop potential values, values in exchange and values in use?"; "Are the beneficiary stakeholders heterogeneous?"; "Is the heterogeneity taken into account in the offer proposition?"; "Do the producing stakeholders

---

[2] Segment by demand supposes that it is the precise knowledge (by survey) of the beneficiaries' expectations which serves as the basis for the offer proposition. In this case, this segmentation is based a priori on expressed expectations or a posteriori on a collection of information on the beneficiaries' behaviors that the offer attempts to facilitate or enrich.

[3] Segment by offer consists in considering that there are no specific elements of identification which make it possible to create a group of beneficiaries predisposed to the proposition and that it is according to the circumstances or the search for variety that whatever beneficiaries will be sensitive to the offer

have information systems associated with the offer allowing them to exploit the property of service inseparability and to reduce the risks created by the extinction of the service (separability)?" and "Are the producing stakeholders able to make beneficiaries the 'premium resources integrators' of the offer proposition by developing value co-creation with these stakeholders?"

All of these issues are for reference only. Chapter 5 that presents the details of the CSV method proposes to analyze the contents of each offer proposition by identifying twelve sensitive points. The examination of each of them allows questioning about the existing offers and their attractiveness. It also leads to reflections on those who can be the object of improvement and innovation.

This fifth step of the TVF method provides the last applicable criteria to the analysis of the general development dynamic of the territory. All the previous stages gradually allow for each theme and all of them to better understand the coherence of the actions under the convergence of the criteria proposed at each stage. Two criteria appear more particularly to characterize the development policy of a territory: the first criterion is that of the means provided (platform, social networks, database or any other means of maintaining contact, etc.) to ensure with the beneficiary, beyond the moment of co-production and contact in the service encounter, monitoring its uses.

These monitoring methods favor a state of inseparability with the beneficiary who, through loyalty, contributes largely to the development dynamics of the theme and by cumulating to the general dynamic of territorial development. This criterion should strongly guide the evaluation of the relational functions analyzed in all stages of the TVF process. The second criterion is used to assess all the forms implemented by the territory to make the beneficiary an actively producing stakeholder in the offer and evolution. The observation here concerns the relational functions that can be implemented to co-create value and to make the beneficiary a "premium resources integrator". The means to be used in the offer proposition to combat the perishability of the offer and ensure co-creation are detailed in Chapter 5.

All the criteria proposed in this step guide the analysts and the political decision-makers towards a specific conception of territorial development. The offer propositions become regulatory elements at the service of governance and its evolution in the TVF. In the offer propositions and the value creation to which they are subject, it is the capacity of governance that is called into question. It is the ability to innovate, in particular, in its relational functions to give truly proactive places and roles to the beneficiary stakeholders. The forms of value creation that drive the TVF are thus inseparable from the forms sought by governance to reduce the tensions between the emergent and the sited.

The objective of this fifth step is to get the analysts to think about territorial development problems from an approach that closely mixes the technical questions of the offers' composition and their acceptability with the strategic questions of governance activities. The last stage of the TVF approach must endeavor to give the territory a coherent and convergent portrait of its development policy. It confronts the feasibility of its options with a particular capacity for the benefit of optimum development. This capacity consists of finding joint and legitimate answers to the technical and normative questions of the offers' contents in regulation and responses to the strategic questions of governance. The conclusion of this book will be used to comment on the lessons to be learned from this sixth step of the TVF method.

6.6 Evaluate the quality of the analysis

Step 6: Evaluate the quality of the analysis (coherence, convergence, feasibility) and the development plan, present in summary the innovations exploitable by the application of the TVF.

All of the first five steps of the TVF process are based on progressive questioning. The questions presented as an indication in Table 6.2 help to accumulate information that should facilitate the synthesis around a central question: "What information must be gathered to obtain a general vision of the capacities of territory to drive its development?" Knowing where to be in order to act gives meaning to this question. The first two stages focus on making the objects of analysis distinctly appear: the territory itself in the first stage or the development themes in the second stage. It is clear that the observers or the policymakers can limit the second step to the analysis of a single or a limited number of themes.

In this case, the analysis of the general dynamic of territorial development and its impact on the theme remains necessary. It provides access to essential determinants of the development policy for the chosen theme(s). Once the scope of investigation and design has been established, the classical logic of looking for opportunities and threats applies. It leads the TVF to carry out synthesis and an initial diagnosis of the territory and its general development dynamic. The analysts are invited to introduce the delicate problem of stakeholders' representations in order to perform their diagnosis. The absence or presence of reasoned formulations on the evolutions of the environment and its new opportunities provide indications on the level of control of the development issues reached by the territory. It is the same for the absence or the presence of strong divergences on the evolution of the offers' contents. The accumulation of observations on all the themes contributes to the first characterization of the development dynamics of the territory.

To deepen the synthesis and draw strategic lessons from it, the third step continues the analytical effort by observing how the stakeholders invest or not invest in the development process. The seven types of dynamics and the eight categories of stakeholders, as well as the relational functions that each of these dynamics develops, express the contribution of the TVF to the evaluation of the development management by the territory. To unravel the complexity of the actors' interplays in the different development dynamics, the TVF method is essentially based on the consistency and convergence of the observations of the first three stages. Coherence and convergence are brought together in the analysis of quantitative information, such as the number of themes of the development plan, dynamics significantly at work in a theme, categories of involved stakeholders, etc., and that of qualitative information, such as the formulation of prospects for future, the nature of the relational functions established by the theme, the nature of the relationships between the decisive stakeholders and other stakeholders, etc. The assessment of the consistency and convergence of observations is thus guided by both a quantitative rule of poverty or wealth (quantity and variety) of descriptors and a qualitative rule of poverty or wealth (the meaning of behavior and nature intentions) observations.

The use of Figure 4.3 on the general dynamic of territorial development suggests avenues to be exploited to conclude that the poverty of quantitative descriptors is often accompanied by the poverty of the production of meaning. The quartiles of introversion and inhibition, like that of immobility, summarize that the small amount of exchanges in relational functions leads to considerable losses of the expressed meaning. Similarly, the quartile of the crisis evokes the poverty of their operational conclusions, regardless of the number of actors mobilized and their exchanges. The consistency and convergence of observations can contribute to the first syntheses on the situation of territory in terms of development. However, the association of the quantitative and qualitative rules of the first three stages must be supported by something other than counting and interpreting intentions and behaviors. The fourth and fifth steps of the TVF method define another rule of consistency and convergence. They explicitly introduce another form of synthesis based on a strategic and operational rule: that of value creation.

These two steps of the TVF method build the diagnosis of territorial development on a single theme: the place and role of the offer's attractiveness in territorial development. The design and implementation of this attractiveness through value propositions do not only concern the offers' contents that embody a theme. The actors, in the design, the realization and the acceptance of the offer, are concerned. The relationships that these actors maintain can, therefore, be analyzed in these three dimensions. The analysts' interest relates to the question of the offer attractiveness and that of the treatment to which it is subject in relations linked to its design, production and acceptance. The analysis is particularly interested in the role reserved for this theme in the reduction of tensions between the emerging and the sited on the MLP axis of governance (listening and taking into account, negotiation, deliberation, conditioned sharing of power, the recognition of legitimacy and so on). All stakeholder exchanges are concerned. The approach affects stakeholders in the governance dynamic and the place and role they leave to value creation for non-decision-makers, all the facilities for its co-production or devices that allow its co-creation. It extends to the stakeholders who bring the resources and combine them as producers or beneficiaries of the offer on the axis of SPT regulation.

At the crossing of the MLP/SPT, the coherence of all the dynamics involved and their convergence on this theme of the offers' attractiveness and their value propositions are at the heart of the TVF's strategic thinking. The diagnosis and evaluation of territorial development applied to governance and regulation is done on this basis. Their relational functions and their practices both on value propositions and their modes of creation build the general synthesis. The driver of territorial development according to the TVF is in this coherence and convergence. To fuel this engine, the place and role of value creation in development are thus designed and exploited for all the reasons presented in the TVF as objects of incessant research for innovation.

Table 6-2: TVF key questions

Steps of Methodology	Some examples of key questions at each step of the TVF methodology
Step 1 Define the territory and its scope of intervention.	-About what territorial entity are we talking? -What identification criteria should be used to avoid making a territorial delimitation error and biasing the analysis?
Step 2 Choose priority themes and their territorial development challenges.	-Are there development opportunities for the territory on the chosen theme? - Is the territory able to exploit these opportunities? -Are any threats weighing in on the exploitation of these opportunities? - Is the territory able to remove it? -Are the territory's policy-makers able to translate these analyzes into strategies?

Step 3 Identify the place and role of stakeholders in each development theme. Select, among the seven development dynamics, those that are active for each theme.	- To which of the eight categories does this stakeholder belong? - What are his properties? -Do the relational factors of the governance dynamic show these stakeholders as decisive or not? -Is there a relational factor for non-decisive stakeholders that links them to governance? -Is it that of negotiation? -What are the categories of stakeholders who drive the opposition dynamic for this theme? -What treatment does the governance dynamic reserve for dormant stakeholders? -Does the notion of non-public exist? -Are the decisive stakeholders capable of restoring the arguments of discretionaries or dependent stakeholders?
Step 4 Diagnose, on each theme, the state of tension (understanding-extension) on the MLP axis (governance). Observe the relational functions implied by the resources of the stakeholders and their combination in the offer propositions on the SPT axis (regulation).	-How, in a territory, the places and roles of stakeholders on a development theme are strengths or weaknesses for this theme? -In what way does the theme escape or undergo the threat of a general incapacity of the territory to conceive the orientations and the objectives or to agree on the technical and normative regime that will make offer propositions attractive? -What are the means and the procedures used by the decisive stakeholders of governance to encourage the emergence of individuals, ideas, innovations? - How do these stakeholders manage to give them a level of extension likely, by way of example or model to follow, to reduce tensions between the particular and the general, the emerging and the sited?-How are these decisive stakeholders able to practice forms of power-sharing or offer sophisticated forms of consultation and co-production of decisions? -Who are the stakeholders directly involved as a "premium resources integrator" or not in providing the resources necessary for the offer proposition? -How do these stakeholders combine their resources in this offer proposition? -What modes of value creation are used? -Do these value creation methods innovate? -Do these modes of value creation solicit and enrich the relational functions of the dynamics concerned? - Does the governance dynamic favor co-creation arrangements?

Step 5 Conceive the most suitable forms of value creation for the offers of each thematic. Evaluate the technical and normative regime(s) ensuring the attractiveness of these propositions on the SPT axis (regulation) using the CSV.	-What are precisely the offer propositions that contribute to the realization of the theme? -Are the stakeholders producing the offer proposition completely identifiable? -What are the values that these stakeholders wish to propose through their offer? -Do the offer proposition statements contain values other than values in use? -Are the beneficiary stakeholders clearly identified? -Are these beneficiary stakeholders identified by segmentation by demand (a priori or a posteriori) or do they fall under segmentation by offer? -Could the integration of other stakeholders' resources enrich the value creation process? -What are the precise contents of the value propositions of the territorial offer? -How does the technical regulatory regime integrate the IHIP properties of territorial offers? -Does the territorial offer develop potential values, values in exchange, values in use? -Are the beneficiary stakeholders heterogeneous? -Is this heterogeneity taken into account in the offer proposition? -Do the producing stakeholders have information systems associated with the offer allowing them to exploit the service properties of inseparability and to reduce the risks created by the service extinction (separability)? -Are the producing stakeholders able, for their satisfaction, to make beneficiaries "premium resources integrators" of the offer proposition by developing co-creation of value with these stakeholders?
Step 6 Evaluate the quality of the analysis (coherence, convergence, feasibility) and of the development plan, present in summary the innovations exploitable by the application of the TVF.	-Does the strategic analysis of the territory cover all of the development themes or some? -Does the information collected provide indications on the level of mastery of development problems reached by the territory, on its knowledge of environmental developments and new opportunities? -Does the information collected reveal divergences in the development of the content of the offers? -Does the analysis enable to clearly approach the general dynamic of the territorial development in one of the quartiles of Figure 4.4?

Lesson to be learned in conclusion of this book	-Do the quantitative and qualitative information gathered on each theme (categories of stakeholders, types of dynamics and relational functions) clearly or approximately confirm the coherence and convergence of the theme with the general dynamic of the territorial development and its allocation to a quartile?
	-How do the relational functions concerning the identified stakeholders appear with decisive stakeholders on each theme and on each dynamic?
	-How do these relationships (negotiation, listening and taking into account, deliberation, sharing of power, recognition of legitimacy, and so on) reduce tensions (emergence and sited) on the MLP axis of governance?
	-Do the relational functions of the dynamics of each theme of the MLP governance axis favor all forms of value creation and, in particular, those of co-creation?
	-What are the relational functions that the governance dynamic maintains with the stakeholders who bring the resources and combine them as producers or beneficiaries of the offer on the axis of the SPT regulation?
	-In a theme and its dynamics, what are the relational functions maintained by stakeholders involved, including beneficiaries, in regulation?
	-How are the offers, by the attractiveness of their value propositions a response of the regulation to the tensions, will be supported by governance?
	-Are the attractiveness of the offers and their value propositions as well as their modes of creation treated by governance and regulation an essential engine of development that conditions all their relational functions?
	-Are the place and the role of value in development conceived and used for all the reasons presented by the TVF as objects of incessant research for innovation?

Bibliography

Felix, M. Ben Mimmoun, S. and Garcia, L. 2021. "The Service Value Cube (SVC): How to make services theories fully usable for service managers" (in reviewing) *Journal of Service theory and practice.*

Lenz, R.T. 1980. "Strategic capability: a concept and a framework for analysis." *Academy of Management Review* 5, 2: pp. 225-234.

Press, G. 1990. "Assessing competitors' business philosophies." *Long Range Planning* 23, 5: pp. 71-75.

Stora, B. 1974. "Firm's environment, towards a theory of contingent decision making." *Management International Review* 114, 1: pp. 105-112.

Weihrich H. 1982. "The TOWS matrix. A tool situational analysis." *Long Range Planning* 15, 2: pp. 54-66.

Chapter 7

Three Case Studies to Put the
TVF Method to the Test

This chapter presents three examples of territory analysis carried out using the tools seen in the chapters 3, 4 and 5. It is a matter of illustrating and commenting on the use of these tools to rethink territorial policies from the Territorial Value Framework (TVF). They are used to apply the six steps of the TVF Method to concrete examples. These three territories present a common desire for development expressed in substantially different contexts. From the available information, each case study presents how the TVF manages to mobilize the tools created in the three preceding chapters. Their application leads to a diagnosis of their respective situation. Based on this diagnosis, three policies emerge which seek to find suitable development solutions and give new perspectives for the future.

The information for these three studies was collected as a part of the VALUES program (Value Analysis of Local Utilities of Enterprises from Social Sector) IRSES Marie Curie project. This collection of information meets the research objectives defined by the European Commission within the framework of its H2020 program (Horizon 2020), conducted from 2012 to 2016. The IRSES project essentially focused on the development of territories from actions and cultural events. This objective guided the collection of data on the theme of culture as an activator of other themes that support territorial development.

To obtain the information necessary for the diagnosis and analysis of these three development strategies, a method of collecting and interpreting the information was adopted. This method is largely qualitative because it seeks to explore the specificities of each territory based in particular on the key questions presented in Chapter 6. The key questions in six stages of the TVF were used as interview grids. They allow collecting data that could be interpreted by the TVF to characterize each development situation and guide future actions in the three territories.

This collection method is carried out in four phases. They promote the description and progressive interpretation of all the dimensions taken by development in the three territories.

The first phase collects secondary or documentary information for internal or external destination delivered by the territories themselves, the press, regional or national institutions (press review on key events in the three territories, activity reports, reports meetings, public presentations of projects, mission letters, scientific journal articles, etc.) In all three cases, the membership of the European VALUES program, the EURALENS association's scientific committee (Le Louvre Lens) and the recommendation of the Soussi University of Rabat facilitated access to internal documents. The information was drawn from an information collection plan focusing on the main TVF questions.

The second phase uses the qualitative focus group method in charge of collecting primary information on the reality and the orientations of territorial development policies. It consists of bringing together four to five stakeholders on the cultural theme of territorial development to reveal the perceived issues, the essential actors and their perceived legitimacy, the pending questions, the developments expected or to be feared.... This phase of exchanges and discussion with a few stakeholders, including beneficiaries, allows defining the contexts, to identify the influential actors and to collect the divergences between the points of view.

The third phase is based on the qualitative technique of the individual interview. From the secondary and primary information collected in the two previous phases, the individual interviews target the influential actors of the territory and seek to confirm the information already collected and to supplement it with the interpretations of these actors. One of the highlights of these individual interviews consists, after explanation, in collecting the opinions and reactions of the interviewed persons based on some of the figures proposed by the three tools of the TVF, the CSV and the stakeholders of chapters 3, 4 and 5.

The fourth phase uses two structural and prospective analysis tools. It is a qualitative phase comprising focus groups and individual interviews with around thirty respondents per territory in order to identify from the TVF, CSV and stakeholders' key variables (chapters 3, 4 and 5) those on which respondents consider it important to act in order to have the most significant effects (impacts). The MICMAC[1] method of structure analysis proposed by Godet (2011) allows this analysis to be carried out quickly using dedicated software. This first step of the process defines where in the games, issues and

---

[1] Méthode d'Impacts Croisés- Multiplication Appliquée à un Classement, this tool is accessible from the following link: http://en.laprospective.fr/methods-of-prospective.html

strategies of the stakeholders are the essential levers for achieving territorial objectives. A second prospective analysis tool is then used: the MACTOR[2] (Godet and Durance 2011).

The objectives of these tools are threefold:

- Decision-making: by researching and identifying the variables and actors on which to act to achieve the set objectives.

- Prospective: by looking for key variables on which reflection should focus as a priority.

- Highlight the evolution of strategic issues and ask key questions for the future.

This fourth step of the collection method provides synthesizable information on respondents' perceptions of the state of a territory, its development dynamic and the practical levers to strengthen it.

Despite this prism of this study, the exercise of the TVF Method retains its external validity and can be generalized to any other development theme, or even open to all the themes that make up the development of a territory. The countries studied in this program are Romania, Morocco and France. Three territories were selected not only for their different and complementary characteristics but also for the development challenges that define the nature of their territoriality.

The first case, on the territory of the metropolitan area of Lille in the north of France, is that of Lille 3000, an organization for the development of cultural events with a tourist vocation. The mission of this development organization is to make Lille a European capital with an international vocation.

The second case concerns the metropolis of Fes in Morocco and the association that supports the annual event of the Festival of Sacred Music of the World, FWSMF. The mission of this association, as it was desired by its founders, is to make this heritage metropolis, traditionally founded on the historical past but not easily accessible to the general public, a territory reviving modernity from the message of opening tolerance and progress of the Arab-Andalusian golden age.

The third case touches on the territory around the city of Lens, located in the former mining basin of northern France and now disused. The case concerns the Euralens organization that is responsible, after the arrival of the Louvre

---

[2] Matrice des Alliances, Conflits, Tactiques & Objectifs entre ces différents acteuRs, this tool is accessible from the following link: http://en.laprospective.fr/methods-of-prospective.html

Museum in Lens, for the territory's economic, social, environmental, and cultural development policy. Territory in total conversion, the conditions for a possible renewal were to be met.

These three cases are of common interest. It is based on the capacity, at the level of each territory and in situations and references to their past so different, to implement a cultural theme capable of initiating the general dynamic of territorial development by creating value for other development themes.

The relevance of the three territories

The structure of these three territories meets the definition of a relevant territory presented in Chapter 1 (cf. 1.1). It offers a coherent framework for a territorial policy and strategy. The relevance of each territory is first defined by the project that is developed there.

Thus, for the territory of Lille, the first case studied in this chapter, the relevance of the territory rests on the construction of the European Metropolis of Lille. It is the metropolitan and urban identity that characterizes this territory in the process of tertiarization and internationalization. The strategy of "think local, act global and act local, think global" takes on all its power. It appears as a perfect illustration of the internationalization of an urban metropolitan territory as presented by Cox (1997, 2011).

The intervention area of the city of Fez, the second area of analysis, is fundamentally geographic and urban. It focuses on the historic medina (old town) which is the city's major vector of attractiveness. If the territorial geography is significant, its identity and its history are also strong defining characteristics of the intervention area: Fez is a former imperial city.

Finally, for the Lens area, the third case study, its territorial strategy is based on a cultural project of the museographic type. Starting from the localized space of the Louvre Museum in Lens, it is the entire institutional territory, represented here by the urban community, which is committed to a territorial development strategy. The very strong identity of this territory, founded on the exploitation of mines, is shaped by a working population, partly of immigrant origin.

7.1 Cases presentation

7.1.1 Case 1: Lille3000 (France)

Figure 7-1: Parade Eldorado lille3000, May 2019

By Damien Troy. (CC BY-SA 4.0, https://creativecommons.org/licenses/by-sa/4.0/deed.en)

In 2004, the city of Lille became the European Capital of Culture. Lille3000 is an organization set up by the city of Lille to take over the organizing committee for cultural events in 2004. Following its designation as the European Capital of Culture, Lille3000's mission, on this momentum, is to maintain the influence of the Lille metropolis beyond this event. This program reflects the political will of the territory to develop not only the European but also the international influence of the city and to strengthen its economic, social and cultural attractiveness. Since 2004, Lille3000 has organized various editions of its cultural program. These editions had provided the following events:

Figure 7-2: Events developed within the framework of Lille3000

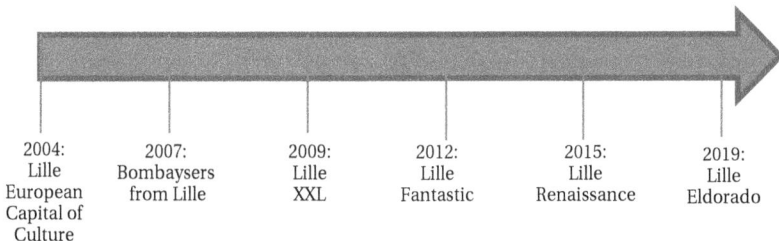

| 2004: Lille European Capital of Culture | 2007: Bombaysers from Lille | 2009: Lille XXL | 2012: Lille Fantastic | 2015: Lille Renaissance | 2019: Lille Eldorado |

Lille was the European Capital of Culture from December 2003 to November 2004 and welcomed more than 9 million visitors. 2,500 cultural events took place during this period. More than 17,000 volunteers had agreed to become "ambassadors" serving as communication and promotion relays in the territory during the year of 2004. Some structures created during this period are places with a cultural vocation located in four districts of the metropolis and are part of the city's cultural landscape.

The mission of the Lille3000 association is to strengthen the influence of the territory and to provoke new impacts that confirm the European and international status of the metropolis. Given the situation of Lille, an industrial city in the north of France, with a low tourist vocation, the mission of Lille3000 is to span several themes of territorial development. Cultural and cultural tourism themes are linked closely to the theme of urban planning and renovation and that of seeking industrial investment, and the quality of life likely to attract high-level executives.

A few years ago, Lille was, above all, a city of "passage" where only business tourism had its place. Cultural tourism was born and has only recently established. This development of cultural tourism is explained not only by the events mentioned above but also by a political will dating from the 1990s and 2000s to renovate many cultural infrastructures. This development strategy associating the theme of culture with that of tourism has extended to the theme of the transformation of urban space in Lille as well as in the metropolis.

This case gives a particularly interesting example of how development themes can impose themselves. The causes can be either that they are priorities to be treated urgently (here, taking advantage of the designation of the city as European capital) and to exploit on in the long term, or that they are vectors of easier and faster development to implement with an appropriate program of events. The declining nature of development themes by exploiting the created synergies can thus be a starting point that includes other dimensions of development swiftly in a more global plan where economy, society and environment have their places.

7.1.2   Case 2: The Fes festival of World Sacred Music (Morocco)

The "Spirit of Fes" Foundation is at the origin of the Fes World Sacred Music Festival (FWSMF). The festival takes place every year in early June. Faouzi Skali, the founder of the FWSMF, defines the objectives of the festival: "I wanted to create a place where people can meet and discover the beauty of each religion and culture. This is what we and the next generation need today, otherwise, we will have a soulless world." In 1991, Faouzi Skali, a scholar and a descendant of a Fassie family, invited ten directors to Morocco to present the films on different spiritual traditions from all over the world.

The event is a success. Even though the songs of the Moroccan religious brotherhoods, afterward, have a greater impact than the films screened. Armed with this experience, the concept of the festival focuses on spiritual music from around the world. It seeks to register as the Forum of Fes in the scholarly, artistic and spiritual tradition of the city. Its first edition took place in 1994. Subsequently, the festival established links with the Fes-Saïss Association, one of the many "non-governmental" regional associations created in the late 1980s and subsidized by the Moroccan government.

Figure 7-3: Performance of Archie Shepp in the 18th edition of the Fes Festival of World Sacred Music.

By Ramon Fornós. (CC BY-SA 3.0, https://creativecommons.org/licenses/by-sa/3.0/deed.en)

Over time, the festival becomes the highlight of the Spirit of Fes Foundation. Each year, the festival welcomes a multitude of artists, who come from all walks of life and all cultures. Concerts take place in the courtyard garden of the Batha Museum, and shows are staged on the grounds of the Bab Makina Palace. The program is as rich as it is varied, combining several innovative artistic forms and contributing to cultural and tourist development. During ten days, various events and evenings take place in all the important monuments and sites of the medina (old town). These events grow year by year and contribute to the international influence of Fes.

Conceived, at the outset, as an opportunity to replace the city of Fes in its historic influence as an imperial city charged with a history of the religious and scholarly center, the festival makes the cultural reference of sacred music the symbolic and concrete starting point of another theme. That of human development expressed in all its forms. The concept of the festival is for these animators a development vector oriented on the cultural, social and economic conditions of contemporary humanism. What makes "the spirit of Fes" is the message of respect for different cultures, their coexistence and mutual enrichment, and the spirit of tolerance. "A universal message of peace and rapprochement between peoples" as the founder of the festival hoped, drawing inspiration from the Arab-Andalusian golden age, whose story reinterpreted made it the precursor of this message.

Again, the theme of cultural development takes its unifying character from other themes of development. They are associated with a strong narrative (the Arab-Andalusian golden age) to give substance to themes, like that of sustainable development. The period of the festival, through the numerous conferences of the Forum, is a vital moment to reaffirm the links between humanism and the sustainable economy.

The cultural theme developed by the festival feeds the subject of economic development through leisure tourism. This hybrid, cultural and economic theme, takes on particular dimensions of development which is authentic artisanship rooted in the tradition of trades or advance of nearby tourist routes. They allow travelers to stay longer and increase the economic benefits of visiting periods. The dynamics of the preceding themes are also relayed by development topics, such as the theme of the restoration of popular housing in the old city animated by the spirit of Fes.

7.1.3 Case 3: Louvre-Lens Museum and Euralens (Hauts de France)

Figure 7-4: Louvre-Lens, Museum in Lens, France.

By George Hodan. (CC0 Public Domain,
https://creativecommons.org/publicdomain/zero/1.0/)

Locating the Louvre in Lens, an average city of 30,000 inhabitants in the heart of an ex-mining region, is the result of a strong desire for decentralization and cultural democratization. It is driven by the management of the Louvre Paris that seeks to develop "branches" outside the capital and by the French government in the general framework of decentralization. In 2003, the French Minister of Culture and Communication launched an appeal for a movement to decentralize large Parisian cultural establishments. In response to this call, the Louvre Museum undertakes to create "another Louvre" in the regions. On November 29, 2004, the President of the French Republic chose Lens as the host site for the new Louvre from six candidate cities.

This project, welcoming and bringing some of the most prestigious art collections to life in the heart of the ex-mining basin, has become a reality thanks to the mobilization of local players, and the commitment of the President of the "Hauts-de-France" Region and the pledge of the mayor of Lens. The region has positioned itself to host the Louvre Museum's decentralization project, agreeing to be the contracting authority and the main sponsor of the construction and operation of the museum. In this context, the choice of Lens appears to be an accessible opportunity. The theme of cultural development with the arrival of the Louvre takes on another dimension thanks to the reputation of the museum. It can help launch other themes for the future of the territory. The subject of urban development, that of economic attractiveness as well as social cohesion linked to the pride of bringing to fruition the candidacy of Lens and of changing the game by returning to strong signs of dynamism and success.

The Louvre Lens project, with its regional, European and international dimensions, is conceived in this triple ambition: cultural, economic and social. The inaugurated was on December 4, 2012, and the museum was open to the public, for the first time, on December 12, 2012. Within the former mining basin, the Louvre-Lens host area benefits from a special geographical position, between the two areas of the cities of Lille and Arras. This triple ambition is entrusted to a development mission called "Euralens", formed as an association in January 2009. Euralens brings together the local authorities, political, economic and social players that host the Louvre. This collegiality aims to found a common and shared vision of the challenges of development and regional planning, and to identify excellent projects that can claim the label of Euralens. The function of this label is to solicit projects from principally local actors and to promote them financially. The award of the label depends on the ability of the projects to fuel development on the themes of culture, economy, society, and environment. The Euralens approach is inspired by experiences from other European countries. In Bilbao, in the Spanish Basque country (Guggenheim Foundation) but also in Liverpool of Great Britain (Tate Museum) and in Ruhr of Germany (Emscher Park). Lens, like these territories, were mining and/or industrial basins and in economic and social difficulties, with unemployment rates higher than the national average. Today, these territories are winning again.

7.2 The application of the TVF Method

7.2.1 Define the territory and its scope of intervention

Step 1: Define the territory and its scope of intervention

Step 1 of the process seeks to define a relevant territory for intervention. The territorial perimeter appears at the intersection of several criteria: geography (physical and human), the living area (where socio-economic and cultural behaviors shape their own identity), and the political and administrative (whose missions depend on the territorial and national organization). Each criterion delimits a territory superimposable on the other delimitations to reveal the relevant territory.

Infrastructure and travel times in the geographic location are important criteria. In the three case studies, there is one thing in common among these three territories: each of them is at the heart of a crossroads of transportation. The European metropolis of Lille is located in the center of a triangle made up of three European capitals that are Paris, London and Brussels. This location is strategic because it is the transit point for the TGV (High-Speed Train) which puts the three European capitals within 1.5 hours from Lille (30 minutes for Brussels, 1 hour for Paris and 1 hour 30 minutes for London). Within a radius of fewer than 480 miles, Lille is thus at the heart of a customer catchment area of 300 million inhabitants.

The city of Fes played a role of capital of the Arab-Andalusian world, connecting the kingdom of Granada to the Rif, in history until the 16th century, even with a few eclipses in between. Its position, away from the administrative (Rabat) and economic (Casablanca) capitals of Morocco, has made it a "sleeping beauty" since the 17th century. From an imperial city, a place of political and economic concentration, it has mainly become a city dedicated to tourism, in particular by the quality of its medina (old city), and its heritage and cultural capital (soil of Sufi culture in Morocco). The tourism component of its development is a part of its strategic positioning and economic future.

The city of Lens, the administrative capital of the former Lens-Liévin mining area, perfectly covers the concept of a living area. As a former flagship of the coal industry, the local landscape had been shaped by mines and their exploitation. With the closure of the pits in the 1970s and 1980s, the basin went through many crises. However, its geographic location is not without interest because it is located in the same customer catchment area as the European Metropolis of Lille. Lens can take advantage of the short and rapid trips available to a dense population if the territory manages to create offers likely to provoke them.

According to the criterion of socio-economic and cultural behavior and that of the dimensions that shape the representations of populations, the situations of the three territories are different. They are in their content but obey the same explanatory variable in all three cases.

This variable is a historical and cultural experience. Regarding the city of Fes, the turbulent history of relations between the Muslim kingdoms of Spain and the Maghreb has founded an Arab-Andalusian identity on a cultural and religious basis. This identity is still alive in modernity because it expresses a golden age. It is the source of pride in belonging which is easily shared on particularly topical values such as tolerance, dialogue and inter-religious coexistence. This identity is all the more mobilizable as it is opposable to what the whole population perceives as the current evils of societies. This identity heritage benefiting from a, sometimes, fantasized story offers an image support that should not be built here but exploited as a heritage.

Figure 7-5: Geographical locations to enhance

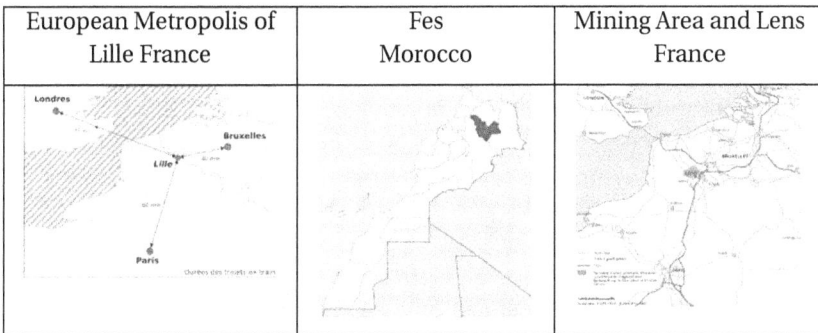

European Metropolis of Lille France	Fes Morocco	Mining Area and Lens France

The Lille metropolis does not offer an identity experience strongly anchored in such a unique and centered historical, cultural and religious reference. The Lille metropolis is a border territory. It is experienced in the commercial exchanges carried by the history of Flanders, a hub between the north (Belgium, the Netherlands and Germany) and the south (Mediterranean countries). These exchanges imply the passages, transfers and mixtures of populations and influences. This history is also responsible for making it a territory of repeated invasions and giving it an experience of the disasters of war creating a strong aspiration for Europe and peace. The advantages to be gained traditionally from exchanges leads this metropolis to favor an international vocation and belonging to a Euroregion shared in particular with Belgian Flanders. This identity prepares this territory, in particular, to desire to reach a critical size allowing it, in the face of these three nearby capitals, to better take its share of the growing exchanges.

The territory of the metropolis of Lens has a paradoxical identity. It is entirely shaped by the mining and working-class culture, the remnant of an entirely vanished world. Faced with this hidden reality, representations of the past stemming from the social organization of economic activity are still present in extremely shared values of solidarity, which are courage in the face of adversity and difficult communication with those who do not share the common experience. The retraining initiatives deemed insufficient to cover the needs for a large and specialized workforce lead the territory to perceive itself as "left behind". Associated with discouragement and the feeling of abandonment, territorial identity, experienced as a loss, finds it difficult to draw on its own references to invent its future and forms of development.

In terms of the administrative delimitations of these three territories, they fairly attach to the local identity factors to which the respective populations refer. These delimitations are not artificial and are a significant element of communication and legitimacy.

For the European Metropolis of Lille and Lille3000, territoriality is purely administrative since it is supported mainly on the territory of the European Metropolis of Lille (EML), then on the Region.

For the city of Fes, the territoriality of FWSMF is that the medina (old city) stepped into history. This medina is renowned for the quality of its urban planning and remains one of the jewels of the Arab-Andalusian culture. In fact, the FWSMF promotes these identity attributes by performing concerts in historic sites (Bab Al Makina, Dar Ardiyel, Dar Mokri, Dar Tazi, Batha Museum, and Bouljoud Place) which allows a complete appropriation of the historical sites for the user.

Finally, for the metropolis of Lens, the use of the administrative variable is based on a double territorial division. The first is based on the site of the museum itself. The latter is located in a concentration area with cultural and sports facilities. This location is chosen on purpose, the museum is located near the football stadium, football being at the heart of Lens traditions. In times of adversity, football becomes a vector of pride in belonging to which the inhabitants of Lens are very sensitive. The proximity of the stadium and the museum, of sport and culture, reflects geographically a real desire for "taming", the neighborhood desired by the architects themselves. The interior of the museum is fully visible from the outside thanks to a glass enclosure. The second territoriality is that of Euralens and the basin of life. Indeed, Euralens is designed as the necessary development tool to extend the establishment of the Louvre. By Euralens and the establishment of the Louvre, a development theme calls for others across the entire living area for promoting economic, cultural, social, and environmental attractiveness.

The relevant territory is often defined as a territory that crosses the geographic, identity and administrative approaches. However, this definition might be incomplete if the logic of the stakeholders and their willingness to initiate a development policy in their territory is not involved. The perimeter of a relevant territory is, therefore, dependent on all these factors. For the three cases, it is noted that the definition of the relevance of the territories is dependent heavily on the identity, the physical and administrative geography of the space and the will to set in motion these territories. This desire is characterized by the FWSMF, the Louvre Lens and Lille3000.

Figure 7-6: Different territorial characteristics

EML Territory in the Department of North in France	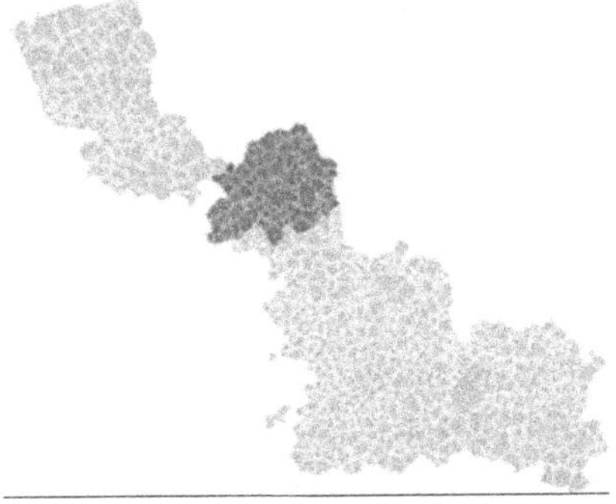
FWSMF in the medina of the city of Fes in Morocco	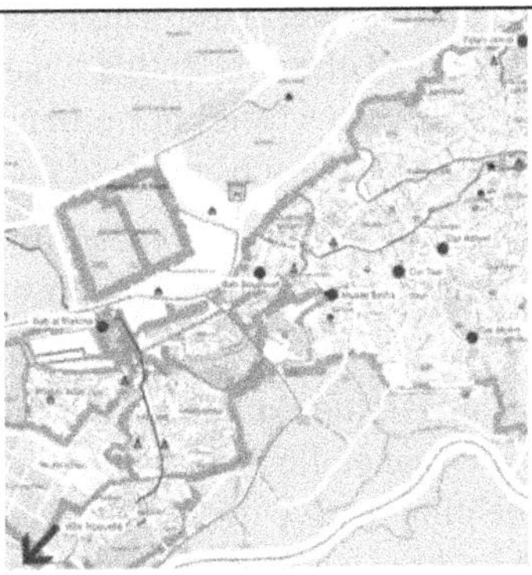
Euralens territory in the former Mining Basin in France	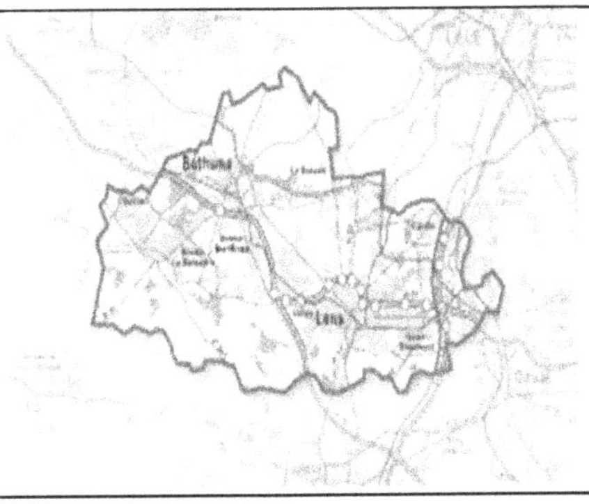

7.2.2 Choice of priority themes and their territorial development challenges

Step 2: Choice of priority themes and their territorial development

Starting from very different situations, the three territories faced an identical problem: reviving the general dynamic of their development. Such a relaunch is particularly difficult when the most favorable development themes, such as tourism for Fes, logistics based on distance trading and E-commerce activities for Lille, or on no specific theme except for industrial tourism based on the discovery of the mining history for Lens, are only able to play a driving role in this general dynamic, to mark a clear ambition from which all development themes can echo.

The first observation was evident: each chosen development theme could represent for each territory a competitive advantage, but, in no case, a key factor of success giving a strong form to a specific skill or knowledge. The promising offers of development existed. None of the three cases did provide personality traits or territorial positioning from which the expected themes of territorial development could be developed in synergy. The second observation revealed how the three territories were unable to deploy the most of a common opportunity: that of being at the heart of geographic areas of intense movement of people and transit of goods. At this stage of the diagnosis, the three territories appeared to be on trajectories of human and commercial exchanges without having the means to take advantage of them and exploit them for their benefit.

Placing elements of attractiveness to take advantage of the benefits of transforming a transit area into a stopover and transaction location became a priority issue.

In such a context, the exploitation of this opportunity required following an essential need: that of the recognition and image of each of the territories. The answer to helping resolve the problem required precise use of the notions of recognition and image. Before the reorientation of their development policy, Fes, Lille and Lens were not known and, especially, not by those who were passing through for business or leisure. None of them enjoyed a reputation and an image capable of influencing on traveling and transaction behavior.

Certainly, the European Metropolis of Lille (EML) was known at the national level or in neighboring countries (Belgium, Netherlands and England). Its image was rather mixed or neutral (interviewees knew the name of the city but had no specific opinion on it).

The city of Fes also suffered from a weak international image. It was not, in itself, a destination with an international vocation and associated in the international attractiveness of Morocco with one of the four former imperial cities. Renowned for its historical heritage, the state of buildings abandonment in the 10,000 alleys of the medina went hand in hand with stagnant tourist attendance till the 1980s.

With regard to the Euralens Mining Basin, the deficit in attractiveness was even greater. The closure of the last mineshafts in a region that was almost entirely devoted to the exploitation of coal has created a vacuum for the lack of economic alternatives to meet the needs. Without an alternative future, development strategies were cautiously presented as attempts to restore the territory and its inhabitants to "resilience". The geographical position of the territory and the industrial reputation, of which little know-how could still be valued, were exploitable opportunities only on one condition: to provide the territory with offer propositions likely to revive the attractiveness and position it in the intensity of the North European traffics somewhat other than a forgotten destination. The statement of this condition alone reinforced, among elected officials and the inhabitants, the feeling of having given a lot (the intensive production of coal for reconstruction after the last world war) and of being left behind, abandoned its weak resources. Even the Lens football team, going into the second division, lost any chance of getting Lens talked about in the national sports media.

From a strategic point of view, the presence of an opportunity (to be in intensive trading areas) that none of the three territories managed to exploit led to a real obstacle. This lock is recognition and image. In all three cases, the two terms were used strategically while avoiding stereotypes. Everyone agreed on two things: being known with all the costly efforts, especially in communication, is not enough. The exploitation of the geographic opportunity must go through strong triggers that give the aimed opportunities to stop on their routes, and better still, to set up stops there to promote and optimize exchanges for their benefit. In exploiting this geographic opportunity, the theme of cultural development has never been treated as an independent theme by the decision-making stakeholders in the three territories.

The three governances, distinguished in their composition, have been able to create relational functions and technical regimes capable of reviving other essential themes of territorial development (the improvement of the habitat, the promotion of the living environment, the mission of prospecting for the international investment, sustainable economy, the revival of know-how, the search for partnerships to densify the territorial offer proposals, etc.). In this, the three governments considered that a simple policy of cultural prestige did not meet the requirements of reviving the dynamics of the development of the territory. The three governances, despite the opposition of certain stakeholders in the name of urgency, have made the cultural theme a priority theme of territorial development by drawing all the lessons from the notion of image that often accompanies that of recognition.

Reputation is not enough, especially if it can be negative like notoriety. This means that the image is strategically inseparable from the notion of "evoked set" (Howard 1969) to play the desired role here. Constructing the image, the entire evoked set deals with the necessary presence of the three cities in the mind of defined targets. This presence in mind is useful and must be linked to specific activity opportunities for the targets (leisure, business destination, search for industrial or logistical establishments, training, etc.)

The strategy, therefore, consists of dealing with the image problem from the opportunities that the three cities have to be present in the choice of target activities through their offer propositions. In all three cases, the territories chose a starting point to be present in the minds of the targets by adopting specific occasions that would call others on other development themes. The most applicable metaphor to this strategy is, according to the mayor of Lille at the time, to seek a theme that serves as a "turbine" conducive to territorial dynamics.

The choice of the "Métropole de Lille" then fell on hosting events. The first one was the EML's candidacy for the 2004 Olympic Games. However, if Lille arrived in the finalist of four cities, it was not retained. This offer, conceived as a multi-site offer with other cities in the eurozone, made it possible to register the city in a cross-border economic and cultural group that was able to compete with the three neighboring capitals. The title of the European Capital of Culture obtained at the same time, as the port of Genoa in Italy, was an opportunity to recall the role of Lille and Flanders in trade relations with the Mediterranean world. The Lille3000 project, with the European capital of culture, is the strategic extension of reflection on all of the actors of economic or cultural mobility in North-West Europe.

Using the same event strategy, Fes was able to perpetuate a festival that immediately became part of other themes than that of cultural action alone. Revisiting the Arab-Andalusian civilization, making it a leitmotif of the territory, allows associating development themes in perfect synergy with all the economic and social concerns of the Maghreb. The training capacity of the cultural theme for development was also used for its capacity for evocation. Putting the territory in a position to be chosen, by giving it a place and a role in selected development scenarios, is the common strategic basis in the three cases.

The special situation of the Euralens forced the territory to follow a different path compared to sharing the same strategy in the other two territories. The critical situation of the territory made the question of the exploitation of geographic opportunity even thornier. The initial observation was that the territory could certainly have a certain national recognition, but it was entirely contained in its past industrial history. As soon as the reflection focused on the place and the role of the territory in the stakeholders' evoked set concerning the occasions to shield it, the arguments ran out or were not able to measure the problems to be resolved.

All the solutions appeared to be insufficient and, therefore, unsatisfactory. Each debate over them fueled uncertainty and crisis. All stakeholders struggled to establish the legitimacy of their solutions. The crisis mainly resulted from the territory's low credibility in defining what the occasions were while it could be a bidder for targets. Expecting to be part of a round of consultation or deliberation on any development activity seemed unrealistic.

For Lens, taking up the problem of initiating the development dynamic through the theme of culture came down to the theme of industrial tourism. It further increased the risks of perception of a poor past. The candidacy for the establishment of the Louvre Museum firstly aroused strong opposition. Given the crisis, what was dealing with is unessential and non-urgent. The fully sited governance (President of the region, prefect of Pas de Calais and the mayor of Lens) brought the candidacy to its success creating a new and particularly interesting situation described in the image strategy in the second stage of the TVF approach.

As in the two preceding cases, the strategy of the Lens territory makes the cultural theme the support of its development dynamic. Cultural attractiveness and its ripple effects on other themes are well explored after. It is completely imported. The attractiveness is created ex nihilo by the complete importation of a prestigious museum and its image. This implantation was perceived by many stakeholders as artificial and not exactly related to a territory marked by work or the history of art. The strategists justify this establishment on a double legitimacy: the right for a working territory, in the name of cultural democratization, to access the most precious forms of artistic heritage and offering the museum a catchment area accessible by highway and/or TGV extended to all of Northern Europe. The Louvre becomes a powerful means of placing Lens in the evoked set of millions of English, Belgian, Dutch, German, or Scandinavian tourists going to the south for their holidays. The offer proposition could justify stopping. This strategy of cultural attractiveness ex nihilo is strongly inspired by the example of Bilbao in Spain and the establishment of the Guggenheim Museum.

In this second stage of the TVF, the three territories have chosen a priority theme for the revival of their development dynamics. This priority theme is culture. And the meaning to be given to this priority has to be examined. According to the TVF, the nature of the threats hanging over many territories may justify the choice of such a priority. Two conditions are, therefore, essential: the first "technical" condition linked to the territory's capacity to apply the rules for constructing recognition and a truly useful and effective image that is associating offer propositions with occasions to use or visit. The second condition of "destination" is linked to territorial accessibility whose desired effects are basically due to the development of travel (individuals and goods) to the territory.

If many threats prevent this construction or this geographic attractiveness, some may contrarily reinforce the choice of such a priority. It is particularly the case for a threat defined in Figure 4.4 concerning the dynamic capacity of territorial development. One hypothesis deserves to be studied. The priority of the cultural theme, under the conditions set out above, is specifically suited to the territories that have to overcome the threats defined in Figure 4.4. The threats of introversion-frustration, immobility and crisis can find resolution strategies in prioritizing the cultural theme.

Figure 7-7 below shows the three cases studied present threats to their general development dynamics.

Figure 7-7: Situation of the three territories with regard to their capacities

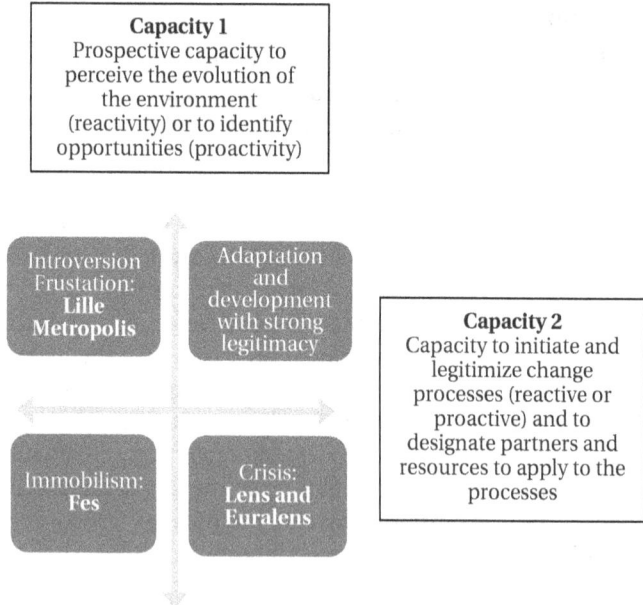

In the three territories, the two conditions known as technical or destination are met, and there is a specific threat for each of them on their ability to initiate a general dynamic of development. The metropolis of Lille is positioned as a territory whose opportunities are clear, inspired by its geographic location that promotes cross-border exchanges in European integration. These are the modes of exploiting these opportunities that find neither the stakeholders nor the combination of resources to meet resolutely the international challenges. These two characteristics make the Lille Metropolis a characteristic example of the quartile of introversion and frustration before the implementation of the new policy. A strong ambition that hardly takes shape and difficulty in seeing the winning practices appear.

Fes, a city where memories of greatness have crumbled, lives its politico-administrative situation as relegation and its cultural and religious references within the limits of community practice. The single expectation of the territory was, above all, to maintain the existing sources of values (crafts, traditional tanneries, etc.) and the fragmented initiatives provided only solutions whose ambitions remained closely corporatist. Transforming the territory into a meeting place for civilizations that restore meanings and truths to them came from a private initiative. It jealously guards, in the Spirit of Fes association, her autonomy to remain available to all and to unite all the wills, without a priori, that fight against immobility.

According to the TVF, the mining basin combined with the most disturbing criteria to boost its dynamic development capacity. The condition of destination could only be satisfied marginally and with reference to the past. The technical conditions for building recognition and image in the targeted geographic area were not met for the absence of expressing opportunities to visit and offer propositions for a real revival. In Figure 7-2, the characteristic threat that weighed on the territory, from the point of view of its general dynamic of development, was indeed the threat of the crisis quartile. The main characteristics of this quartile are present: a depressing projection into the future, without a motivating and legitimate formulation of its ability to exploit the geographic area of European trade and transit, and incessant debates on offer propositions that are unable to meet the two conditions above. Only has the transfer of the spectacular value proposition from the Louvre Paris to the Louvre Lens opened a way out of the crisis.

The examples of these three territories have highlighted the strategic TVF grid and its use to relaunch a territorial dynamic of development. This reading grid in this second stage enables us to select development opportunities by clearly associating the question of the place and the role of the territory in its exploitation over a long period. If this operation meets the condition of destination and attractiveness that gives meanings to the term "territory", it is possible to select one or more priority themes, and then ask the question of the "technical" condition to build awareness and image. Finally, the problem of threats to the territory can extend to the specific threat of the dynamic capacity of the territory. The diagnosis of this threat, as proposed by the three analyzed situations, can be employed to make the strategic choice of the priority development theme.

7.2.3 Identify the places and roles of stakeholders in each development theme.

Step3: Identify the places and roles of stakeholders in each development theme. Select, among the seven development dynamics, those that are active for each theme.

In this stage of the TVF methodology, the first step is to identify the stakeholders present in the design and implementation of the theme. To limit the analysis, this inventory mainly concerns the priority theme and themes that can benefit from its impact. Each case is treated successively over the two phases (inventory and functional analysis) of this third stage. The analysis must not only identify each stakeholder but try to characterize it according to the eight categories specified in Figure 4.2 and their properties in Table 4.1. The questions to be retained relate to the belonging to a stakeholder in one of the eight categories and the properties it possesses in terms of power, legitimacy and the urgency of its requests.

Regarding the territory of the Lille Metropolis, the stakeholders who are likely to interact in the design and implementation of the priority theme and the themes benefiting from its spinoffs can be presented according to Table 7-1 below:

Table 7-1: Lille Stakeholders' analysis

Criterion	*Stakeholders*
Decisive	Mayor of Lille
Dominant	Lille3000
Dependent	Local operators of cultural activities
Dangerous	Certain artists and cultural operators who fear a commercialization of culture
Dormant	
Discretionary	Cultural development structures and cultural operators
Demanding	The inhabitants of the metropolis and the "ambassadors" (volunteers)
Non stakeholders	Non-public, those who do not participate

The cultural theme supported by Lille3000, along with all the themes presented as potential beneficiaries, brings a relatively small number of stakeholders together. However, seven categories of stakeholders are identifiable. They show the possible complexity of the relational functions that are established on this theme according to the involved dynamics. The dynamics of governance and that of decision are more important since they have the role of strong initiative here. The privilege given to events of international dimension, such as the Olympic Games, European Capital of Culture, etc., explains this situation. The dynamics of expertise and legitimacy are the echoes of a regularly strong dynamic: opposition. The offers mainly concerned international events, the consequences of which were sometimes disputed (residents' taxes or traffic difficulties relating to the games). The dynamic of the opposition often gathered stakeholders (discretionary or even "dangerous") advocating a socio-cultural and emancipatory vision of the culture rooted in the territory and opposing the "media culture". In this situation, the dynamic of expertise becomes a precious reinforcement to develop an argument, particularly in relation to discretionary stakeholders who have strong legitimacy. The functional analysis of all these actors and those of the relational functions established among these different dynamics is crucial to ensure the most widely agreed development dynamic.

The situation of the stakeholders according to their category for the territory of Fes is presented below in Table 7-2:

Table 7-2: Fes stakeholders' analysis

Criterion	*Stakeholders*
Decisive	Fes Saïss
Dominant	Spirit of Fes Association
Dependent	Local structures for welcoming festival-goers (hotels, guesthouses, etc.)
Dangerous	
Dormant	Local elected officials
Discretionary	Local tourism operators
Demanding	
Non Stakeholders	Paradoxically, the Fassis can be involved in the process before the development of popular actions on Bouljoud Place.

The theme of the cultural development of Fes linked to the Festival of Sacred World Music has its starting point in a purely private initiative based on the provision of personal resources and good interpersonal skills. This explains why, despite the general ambition of the project, a few stakeholders are directly involved by the approach. Consequently, in the implementation of this theme, local elected officials or city authorities and local representations of the state are classified among the so-called "dormant" stakeholders.

The role of Fes Saïss is to ensure the future of the festival and the progressive integration of partners in a highly autonomous manner. These are, in particular, the discretionaries who are entrusted with missions that allow the growing reception of tourists and festival-goers and the enrichment of local offers in crafts and services. Likewise, dependent stakeholders come into and play as providers who understand the benefits of the city's new reputation. The "carte blanche" phenomenon left to the initiators makes it possible to obtain aids without compensation in terms of governance. To maintain this exclusivity, the dynamics of governance and decision-making concern a few individuals, often from the same family group or from co-opted relationships, acting with prudence for the benefit of the city and the festival in "enlightened" managers.

The dynamic of legitimacy is entirely assumed by the pioneering status of Fes Saïss. It essentially establishes its relational functions as the principal with stakeholders. Above all, it plays this role with the stakeholders of the technical regime, so-called "dependent", for the implementation of the festival or the support for tourism development. The "Spirit of Fes" defines the dynamic of education and communication, and the relational functions of this dynamic with governance are part of the scrupulous respect for this spirit. The city of Fes, since the start of the festival, has benefited from two investment programs of state for its renovation. This "parallel" implication is achieved without any direct intervention of the state in the dynamic of governance and decision of Fes Saïss which acts, so far, as the most legitimate entity to take charge of the theme of cultural development and the other beneficiary themes for the benefit of the territory. This difficult balance to this point likely between the "guardians of the recognition of Fes and the brand- Festival of World Sacred Music" and the sited governance of the territory appears to be a particularly original point in the life of the MLP in this territory.

For the Lens territory, during the period of the strategic choice of the Louvre Museum implementation in Lens, the main identifiable stakeholders were distributed according to the following categories in Table 7-3:

Table 7-3: Lens stakeholders' analysis

Criterion	*Stakeholders*
Decisive	President of the regional council and prefect of department, town hall of Lens
Dominant	Local technicians (Mission Bassin minier, technicians from Public establishments of Intercommunal Cooperation), local elected representatives of the main agglomerations of the metropolis
Dependent	Local development associations and stakeholders in town planning
Dangerous	Certain categories of inhabitants who consider that the coming of the Louvre in Lens is not adapted to the local context
Dormant	Local elected officials from 36 municipalities in the territory
Discretionary	Tourism development structures
Demanding	The Chamber of Trades and Craftsmen Associations, the Chamber of Commerce
Non Stakeholders	The inhabitants of the Lens area, the chamber of agriculture

The stakeholders involved in the implementation of the Louvre in Lens and the creation of Euralens are quite a few. Given the fact that only the dynamics of governance and expertise were intensely mobilized for setting up the project in the record time (45 days), a large number of these stakeholders did not participate in these two dynamics. The establishment of the museum required a government agreement and it was obtained by stakeholders at the highest level of regional authorities (the Presidency of the Region, the prefecture, the sub-prefecture, and the mayor of Lens) in a select committee.

The dynamics of governance included a few protagonists who were responsible for putting the nomination file together and using their influence on the French Ministry of Culture or the management of the Louvre Paris. Under these circumstances, the relational functions of governance were extremely narrow with the dynamic of expertise on which the quality of the application file depended. The dynamic of decision in the region was limited to making every effort to have the file selected after a competition with other territories. As a result, only stakeholders with power, legitimacy and the capacity to deal with the emergency involved in the decision-making process. They have forged close ties in this veritable "commando operation" with stakeholders in the expertise dynamic. The decision to set up, coming from

Paris, forced the stakeholders to carry out the project to reinvent new relational functions with all the other stakeholders of the territory and relaunch the dynamics of governance and decision in the long term. The announcement of the museum's arrival overturned the governance and decision-making dynamics inherited in part from the period when the mining companies and then the coal mines of France ensured a great influence on the management of the territory. The reinvention and revival of governance, which is no longer based on a "steeple spirit" favored by the fragmentation of the territory left from mining concessions, was expected to be delicate. The functional approach proposed by the TVF allows, in the continuation of this third step, showing how, in an original way, the reintegration of the stakeholders who did not participate in the assembly of the file modified the traditional relational functions and integrated new dynamics around the theme of the cultural development of the territory.

In this third stage of the analysis of the TVF, the inventory of the stakeholders involved in the development theme is followed by the functional analysis of their roles. This functional analysis questions the relational functions of these actors according to the dynamics sought. The TVF approach proposes to conduct this analysis, paying particular attention to the relational functions that are established in the dynamic of governance among all stakeholders and extend to regulation.

In the example of the Lille Metropolis, the management of major successive events (the Olympic Games, European Capital of Culture and Lille3000), sources of the conquest of regional and international partnerships, was accompanied by a desire, "throughout a territory, to innovate, to find another way of experiencing culture in its relations to education, sports, living environment, transport, town and country planning, urban practices, and news solidarity". These major founding events were the result of strong governance, relatively concentrated around a measured number of decision-making stakeholders with the power of initiatives and sufficient legitimacy to implement them. The desire to obtain significant socio-cultural and economic benefits over the long term has strengthened the relational functions of this governance dynamic towards non-decision-making stakeholders. The establishment of the Euralille spatial planning tool has played a part in this.

In this context, the search for the desired extensions of the cultural theme to beneficiary themes gave birth to the Lille3000 association. Its mission is to make an event program every two years and to allow governance open to new stakeholders who were not originally decision-makers. Lille3000 ensures its autonomy and acts as a long-term integrator of new internal or external players to the territory capable of ensuring the interfaces of culture with education, transport, the living environment, and so on, and being the operators for the organization and implementation of future events. Lille3000 offers a noteworthy example of governance that seeks to delegate to reinforce the dynamic of territorial development by ensuring, on both the MLP axis and the SPT, communication, coordination and concertation processes, or even negotiation which enriched the relational functions between emergent and sited.

For the territory of Fes, in a different context, the development dynamic on the cultural theme is established at the outset on a pattern close to the metropolis of Lille. The impetus given to the dynamics of governance and decision comes originally from the "Spirit of Fes" association, which brings together stakeholders in the field of expertise and from the Fes Saïss association, which oversees the theme of cultural development for the territory. However, this piloting has not, for the moment, called for revisiting the relational functions of this dynamics of governance and expertise with the other stakeholders of the territory. The governance of the festival is in a position to boost the dynamics of territorial development by coexisting with other regional or governmental governance in a division of roles between the cultural theme and the others, between the medina and the new city. This particular situation means that on the cultural theme, many actors of beneficiary themes are in a position of dormant, dependent or even discretionary.

The permanent and highly specialized nature of World Sacred Music thought and animated, in its dynamics of governance and decision, by people of culture can explain this relatively separate organization of relational functions in the different themes of development. Because the local public actors validate the World Sacred Music as playing perfectly its role in the recognition and the image of the territory, they consider that their field of intervention essentially boils down to making it bear fruit through the engineering of tourism hospitality without seeking a socio-cultural resonance that would go beyond the propositions for more popular shows on Bouljoud Place during the festival.

The situation of the Lens territory is the third example of how a cultural theme can contribute to the general dynamics of territorial development. The functional analysis of the TVF shows how the stakeholders, in the dynamic of governance, can develop their relational functions to strengthen territorial development on all of the beneficiary themes. This planned evolution for development is made necessary by the constitution of the museum's application file. At the outset, only were the dynamics of governance and that of expertise called upon. The decision to locate did not revert to the territory. This dependence determined governance to wait for the end of the competition to launch a real action plan. It engages the dynamic of communication and education (creation of the Project House) to demonstrate other non-decision-making stakeholders who are, nevertheless, highly dominant, and show, for some of them, how this establishment should be exploited for the benefit of beneficial themes such as education, urban planning, the environment, investment, the revival of local trade, etc. It was a question of presenting and doing so that the arrival of the museum is the starting point for a metamorphosis of the territory. These included the emergence of a real metropolis in the mining basin. It must come out of the modes of governance that are often occupied in perpetuating the practices of the past and little awareness of the challenges of urban restructuring. The Parisian decision taken, the will of the decision-makers on the territory, was to make the museum "a springboard to bounce back better". The Louvre Museum aims to be a link in the chain that links the territory's political, social and economic forces in real synergy. The implementation of this revolution in relational functions between the dynamics of governance and decision-making puts power and legitimacy at the heart of the issues.

A new legitimacy is created, in fact, by all the technical problems and the coordination of development projects to be resolved to exploit the museum installation. Likewise, the requirement of territorial metropolisation and urban restructuring oblige local elected officials to admit the benefits of the centrality of the city of Lens, if only to attract visitors to the museum. The Euralens association is created to ensure these changes and organize a coherent and shared economic development project. Memberships of the Euralens association, particularly elected dominant or dormant stakeholders, change the relational functions between the dynamics of opposition, governance and decision-making, and allow the dynamic of expertise to expand with the contribution of international professionals, architects, urban and country planners. The Euralens association also brings about new relational functions with stakeholders in the territory, mainly dormant, discretionary, dependent or non-stakeholder (public). The dynamic of information and education occupies a large part of the activities of Euralens adding to the "Project House", the guided tours of the site and the "cafe of the neighbors" where the actors of the territory meet the inhabitants.

The third stage of the TVF approach, based on the concepts used (development dynamics, categories of stakeholders, relational function, the MLP/SPT axes, and value propositions), establishes under what conditions and at the cost of which changes a territory can accelerate and perpetuate its general development dynamic. In the three cases studied, the cultural theme is chosen to relaunch development. It is in the nature and number of the dynamics and in the relational functions between the stakeholders and the changes they undertake that all the measures taken by the territory can be read to optimize this development and favor the diagnosis of policymakers on what remains to be done.

7.2.4 Diagnose, on each theme, the state of tension

Step 4 Diagnose, on each theme, the state of tension (understanding-extension) on the MLP axis. Observe the relational functions implied by the resources of the stakeholders and their combination in the offer propositions on the SPT axis.

Step 4 seeks to establish, by census and functional analysis, what are the dynamics involved in a theme of territorial development in relation to those of governance and decision-making. It identifies the concerned stakeholders and the relational functions they maintain in these dynamics. The analysts can draw, from this examination, an evaluation of the management mode of each observed theme and tell its evolution and new perspectives for prospect plans. The four quartiles in Figure 4.1 provide a useful point of view on the threats that may weigh on the dynamics of the theme, seek possible techniques to deal with them, and move towards a dynamic "adapted and with strong legitimacy" in its governance and its regulation.

Moreover, the fourth step opens the way to an interpretation of the MLP and SPT axes. It is a concern about analyzing the contents of the relational functions between the emergent and the sited in each topic. These contents give access to the state of the tensions between understanding and extension on the MLP and SPT axes. These two axes carry the tensions and their forms of resolution between two types of stakeholders. The first type expresses the individual experience, namely local point of view, in its specific practices, initiative and spontaneous innovation.

The second type is likely to be a spirit of innovation or initiatives. It represents the decisive stakeholders in governance and decision leading or delegating the regulatory axis in which the offers take shape. Through this approach, the fourth stage of the TVF assesses how the dynamic of the theme is or is not under tension regarding the legitimacy and the response to the urgency of the theme.

The analyses of the three case studies through the TVF show different and complementary situations. These are characterized by different levels of capacity (extension, understanding and decision-making) which act on the very structuring of the profile of each case. The choice was made to separate the Louvre Lens study into two distinct and complementary approaches. Indeed, if the Louvre Lens constitutes the high point of the development activities carried by the territorial political authorities (region, department and prefecture), it is clear that the joint action undertaken by the Euralens association constitutes the dimension of social-economic development and regional planning. Each of the cases presents development approaches and offer propositions that are based on Bottom-Up and Top-Down practices (the MLP). Each requires an analysis of how initiatives are expressed and a consideration of the system for finalizing and accepting offers (the SPT). The approach includes development actions originating from the local initiative or carried out by delegated or non-delegated institutions to compensate for the deficiency of decision-making capacity. The profile of each territory is presented in the following table:

Table 7-4: The TVF profile of the three territories

WSMFF Case: Autonomous and supported development (Bottom-up Vision)	Lille 3000 Case: Territorial development from global governance (Top-down Vision)	Louvre Lens Case: Delegated thematic territorial development	Euralens Case: Delegated and not specialized territorial development

In the three territorial examples, the theme of cultural development allows the observation of these tensions on both axes. The MLP/SPT tension could oppose a "media" culture (Fez, Lille) or an "imported" culture (Lens) to a culture of "socio-cultural activities". In each case, the origin of the initiative is diverse. Resulting from a popular initiative (an initiative of two academics in love with the rich heritage of their city) with regard to the WSMFF, the stakeholders are then aggregated around this approach to make it an event that covers the entire city. More specifically, this event enhances the architectural heritage of the medina by associating it with sacred music. This is how all the cultural players and the cultural and architectural facilities are mobilized for the realization of this event. In addition, municipal services, and in particular the town planning department, act on request as technical support. It is remarkable that the local authority, as an institution, is invested a little in performing this initiative. The relay of the two academics behind this initiative is through the association Fes Saïss and the Spirit of Fes Foundation. This situation illustrates an autonomous and supported development according to a Bottom-Up vision.

The situation is somewhat different as far as Lille3000 is concerned. Started from the initiative of EML (European Metropolis of Lille), the latter is purely institutional, of the centralized type and the order of Top-Down. The strategic objective is to make the city of Lille a European capital with an international vocation. The positioning strategy of the community is structured on tourism and cultural development from a recurring cultural event that takes place throughout the territory of the EML. The action is developed, on the initiative of the community, with the help of the services of the EML and the local authorities that constitute it. These communities provide infrastructure and logistical support in running the various Lille3000 events. The project is delegated to the Lille3000 association. It sets up a set of specific regulations for the event while organizing a mode of governance of the institutional type where the main stakeholders of the territory and the thematic are represented. The popular initiative has little place, even if the demonstration is intended to be popular. For the Lille metropolitan area, initiatives on the subject were strongly sited with the objective of bringing Lille into a network of international partnerships. To meet the conditions of recognition and image, the theme adopts a "media and event culture" mode. The dynamic of opposition took place rapidly on the socio-cultural mode of the culture of proximity and emancipation, the means of which were absent in the face of the costs deemed to be sumptuous of major candidates (the Olympic Games and European capital) and events.

In the case of the Louvre Lens, two keys to read for the TVF can be used to understand the whole approach. The two typologies of the TVF refer to the implementation of an intermediation logic allowing the development of local initiatives while maintaining an institutional framework system. It is the axis of the delegation promoted here: the thematic cultural delegation, for the Louvre Lens, and the normative delegation for Euralens. These delegations of development of local initiatives are explained by the long period of economic and social mourning that the territory experienced following the closure of the mines. The absence of institutional leadership has resulted in technical ownership of the territory based on the quest for legitimacy in terms of economic and social development.

Institutional support exists, but it only concerns the setting up of the project. On the other hand, local communities are inadequately present in the setting up of this project. The approach is more technical and constantly search for legitimacy, since one of the largest museums in the world is located in a popular and deprived territory. The goal is to create a double shock. The first is to make culture accessible to local populations who are often far from it. The second seeks an approach for economic and social development stimulated by young development technicians who are newly arrived at the heart of local economic and social development authorities and represented within the Euralens. Admittedly, the elected representatives of the territorial collectivities and representatives of the Euralens territory are present in the governance of

Euralens, notably in the dynamic of decision. But it is the territorial technical bodies, which bear the legitimacy of the project and which are in support of the development of local initiatives. The origin of the initiative and expansion among stakeholders leads to the request of the articulation between the Top-down and the Bottom-up, and particularly those linked to the management of pressures between the different abilities present in the territory (ability to extend, to understand and make decisions). The use of the Euralens label gives a precious means of articulation to plan a resolution that fits the best to these tensions.

The FWSMF offers a Bottom-up approach where the stakeholders at the origin of the FWSMF are not institutional. They are of the emerging type and generate emerging regulatory processes. To begin with, the FWSMF mobilized a few stakeholders, forming emerging governance that did not involve decision-makers from territorial, regional or national authorities. And then, based on a person's relationships and address book, the regulation was emerging there. The cultural theme of development, inspired by the learned culture and tastes of an intellectual elite, full of the legitimacy of knowledge and taste, does not naturally find its point of balance with popular cultural expectations and practices.

Therefore, the association Fes Saïss and the foundation Spirit of Fes show an important ability for an extension by seeking to position the FWSMF as a real common good for the city and its inhabitants. The forward-looking vision of these organizations is to return the city to its splendor of the Arab-Andalusian capital. It is on this vision on which the legitimacy of the action is based but also the urgency of the latter with regard to the need for positioning of the city. In return, the city of Fes, at the institutional level, shows the weakness for understanding. Admittedly, the FWSMF is vital for the attractiveness of Fes, but its involvement remains pale. This situation shows that the decision-making ability in the case of the FWSMF is not owned by the community but by the structures in charge of organizing the festival. It underlines an extremely robust autonomy of the concerned associations as well as a strong value of power.

The Top-down approach applied by Lille3000 shows a situation opposite to which was present by the FWSMF. The community has demonstrated a capacity for maximum extension in the sense that the approach proposed by Lille3000 tries to generalize the effects of the events carried out within its framework on all local stakeholders. It is a holistic vision of development offered to the entire territory with a real prospect of international positioning. The involvement of residents is only partial. Indeed, the framework for participation is formal and leaves a few initiatives to the inhabitants. It is local and international artists involved in the cultural events of Lille3000 who propose initiatives. They must demonstrate strength for understanding by responding, in a partial way, to the expectations of Lille3000. Thus, decision-making ability is intensely anchored in the institutional framework.

The case of Louvre Lens and Euralens is characterized by a weak capacity for initiative and a fragmented decision-making framework. The territory expresses the need for an offer proposition that is legitimate and responds to the urgency of the situation, but in the absence of decision-making capacity, the territory remains in long-lasting mourning. The legitimacy of the Louvre's location in the heart of the city of Lens expresses the need to find an external solution to the perpetual tension in a territory in crisis. It is through a quest for legitimacy that the later begins its development. The coming of the Louvre has an expected effect of territorial "electroshock" through the mobilization of stakeholders. This mobilization crystallized within the Euralens association. With a relatively frail decision-making ability, the association expresses its power of influence through the acquired territorial legitimacy and the urgency to which it wants to respond. It acts as an intermediary and facilitator between project leaders and decision-making parties. The modes of territorial development presented above ease to sketch out the specific profiles of each territory concerning the four criteria presented in Chapter 3.

C1: Governance and Stakeholders

The governance of the FWSMF is of an associative type. It mainly brings together the stakeholders of the developed cultural theme. For Lille3000, governance is centralized and institutional in nature. However, the governance of the cultural theme concerns the stakeholders in charge of the operational implementation of the project. With regard to the Louvre Lens, governance is delegated and mobilizes the internal and external stakeholders in the territory but involved in the cultural museographic theme (i.e., Louvre Paris). The governance of Euralens is of a normative type. However, its decision-making capacity is centralized in the association's board of directors and at the heart of the decision-making systems of each concerned municipality. Euralens is designed as a place for consultation of all stakeholders with those of governance and decision-making. At this point, the reinvention of relational functions is considered essential for the economic, social and environmental transformation of the territory. Euralens becomes a place of governance and regulation, for "a federation of projects linked together". It should favor a coherent and shared project for the overall development of the territory. The association is responsible for the operational coordination of all actions likely to "bounce back" from the induced effects of the museum establishment.

Euralens, as an association, allows the free adhesion of all the stakeholders involved in the different dynamics of development. This commitment to joint projects allows partners to co-produce value. The Euralens label contributes to the reduction of tensions between the ascendant and the descendant. It is inspired by the logic of co-creation of value, since the label stimulates projects on the part of the inhabitants, as economic or cultural actors, elects them and then finances them according to their contribution to the achievement of one of the development themes of the territory. These themes touch upon culture, the centrality of the territory for the benefit of the accessibility of the museum, the tourist offer and, especially, the extension of the duration of tourists' stays by the creation of guided tours in the mining basin, certified by the United Nations Educational, Scientific, and Cultural Organization (UNESCO), to centers of excellence in the metropolitan development plan.

C2: Regulation and resources combination

The development project led by the FWSMF is based on the need to regulate the functioning of the festival during its realization. This does not only call for a logistical support system but also focuses on the urban revaluation of the medina. It proposes an urban and real estate renovation thanks to a program of de-densification of the medina and renovation of certain Riads, to transform them into guest rooms.

Within the framework of Lille3000, the axis of regulation is fundamental since it is a part of the very objectives of the development project posed by Lille3000. The regulation mainly mentions the image and attractiveness of EML at European and global level. Thereafter, the EML took advantage of Lille3000 to develop its positioning as the capital of culture (the development of the Folies houses, the promotion of the museographic heritage, etc.). This regulatory approach is fully institutionalized and supported by the technical services of the concerned communities.

Concerning the Louvre Lens and Euralens cases, regulation is more technical. The idea is to establish and enhance cultural facilities in the heart of a "disadvantageous" area, to develop accessibility and visibility. The problem for Euralens is almost the same since it is important to combine all of the local resources to set up projects with a sustainable vocation (economic, environmental, social, and developmental). This combination of resources requires the implementation of this interface that is Euralens to allow synergy and involvement of stakeholders on the definition of a proposal for a shared offer through projects to be developed.

C3: Ability to diversify the forms of value creation

The FWSMF was firstly specialized in the promotion of World Sacred Music, rather reserved for an audience of initiates and in prestigious settings (Dar Mokri, Bab Al Makina and Dar Ardiyel). The festival knew how to do evolve its offer regarding the needs and expectations of stakeholders. The successive integration of places of debate on the Arab-Andalusian culture (cultural meetings proposed within the walls of the Batha museum), and then the diversification of performance scenes which open to more popular and less elitist culture (for example, the open stage free of charge at Boujloud Place), or to more local culture (for example, the Sufi nights at Place Dar Tazi) allowed to integrate the local population into this international festival. This adaptation is mainly a function of the ability of managers to perceive the expectations and needs of the local population and to make offers that are adapted. The process of co-production or even co-creation of value remains marginal, despite the involvement of the various stakeholders in these events.

Regarding the case of Lille3000, if the approach is more of the Top-down type, it should be noted that co-production and co-creation of value are very present. Local people are invited to participate in the grand opening parade of each event. For this, preparatory workshops are organized over a year to ensure the participation. Also, the involvement of residents is strongly solicited throughout the event by a number of street shows or simply by the exhibition of artworks in different districts and places of the metropolis. Thus, participation is effective, whether voluntary or not.

For the Louvre Lens, it is through the temporary exhibition that develops this ability to diversify the forms of value creation. In addition, the structuring of the museography, organized according to a temporal and thematic approach, implies more active participation from visitors. Finally, the opening of the museum to the city results in a set of picture windows that open onto a garden where local joggers run regularly. It is clear that this organization is trying to translate a real integration, not only urban but also social, of the museum in the city. With regard to Euralens, the diversification of forms of value creation leads to a label that enables initiative holders to register their project(s) in the dynamic of Euralens.

C4: Methods of resolution of the tension between the informal emergence and the sited institution

The FWSMF is a local initiative that benefits the community. It is technically (logistically) supported by the latter, but is not valued per se. The tensions between the emerging and the institutional are relatively low, and there is a total delegation of the event management capacity to the association who is responsible for it. The community comes in support, but not in portage or co-portage.

The situation is different for Lille3000, which bases its operation on approaches negotiated with the artists, and on the active participation of locals and visitors. The local authority is positioned as active support for the actions carried out by the stakeholders if these fall within the framework defined by the Lille3000 association. There is, therefore, an operational and technical delegation from the community to the association to ensure the setting up of projects as well as their implementation.

For the Louvre Lens and Euralens, it is the delegating approach that manages this tension, especially because this tension is low caused by a weakness of the emerging local initiative and the decision-making ability. In this case, there is a feeble ability for understanding and extension. It is thus the technical approach that generates initiatives and decisions. In the examples of Lille and Lens, the two metropolises have set up mediation parties to support and amplify the reorientation of relational functions among all stakeholders in the territory and that of governance and regulation. These mediation parties as well as the labels (such as Euralens) ease to adapt the development to non-decisive stakeholders, to open up to all the dynamics of the theme, and to enrich their relational functions for strengthening the legitimacy of the actions undertaken.

7.2.5 Conceive the most suitable forms of value creation

Step 5: Conceive the most suitable forms of value creation for the offers of each thematic. Evaluate the technical and normative regime(s) ensuring the attractiveness of these propositions on the SPT axis using the CSV.

In the fifth step of the TVF approach, the analysts assess how the offer propositions for a development theme are able to create values that are the source of their attractiveness. To apply this approach, the TVF proposes to use the CSV (Consumer Service Value) developed in Chapter 5. This step requires having very precise information on how the service is rendered to the beneficiary and knowing the route composed of a before-, during- and after-service. The CSV even encourages providers to question the improvement of the twelve sensitive points of this route to optimize, at a specific time, the process of creating values in each offer proposition.

In the three cases presented, three offer propositions were chosen to illustrate the cultural theme of territorial development: the "fantastic" event within the framework of Lille3000 which offers a course of artistic animation through the city for three days, associating all the major cultural structures and artistic formations of the Metropolis; the Festival of World Sacred Music and the Louvre Museum in Lens. As service offers, the subject of the CSV method, they provide, here, an overview of the questions that drive the responsible stakeholders with the beneficiaries to combine their resources to obtain services rendered with optimum values. These questions give concrete expression to the regulatory activities that drive the relational functions between the stakeholders who are responsible for proposing offers. These questions also concern the dynamics of governance and decision. They drive relational functions of governance and decision-making dynamics, sometimes, in the form of debates.

The CSV, as a method of questioning the design of these offers and their necessary attractiveness, feeds governance into strategic solutions to spur stakeholder satisfaction and a level of tension on the MLP/SPT axes favorable to development. The objective of the presentation of this fifth step is essentially to provide examples of questions raised by the three offers selected in the application of the CSV. The precise use of the complete method refers to Chapter 5 of this book. Without being able to thoroughly examine, for each of the three examples, the twelve sensitive points proposed by the CSV method, this fifth step selects, by way of examples, some of the most strategic points. The first one concerns the treatment of the intangibility of the service offer. Intangibility is linked to the difficulty for all stakeholders, in particular beneficiaries, of representing the offer proposition and why it is desirable, as well as the way the service is delivered and the use values to be expected. In the conception of an offer, concretizing the theme of territorial cultural development (cultural events, museum and festival), governance and regulation must create tangibility and give the offer its potential value. This is more necessary since the cultural initiatives of the three examples seek to fulfill the conditions of recognition and image and to be part of the evoked set of targets.

In the design of the fantastic event, Lille3000, treated the strong intangibility of an event over three days by creating a system where many audiences were urgently requested to become actors of the event (costume manufacturing on-site, excavations organized for children preparing for the event, concerted programming, installation well in advance on main streets of the characters of the parade, etc.). The potential values delivered before the event encouraged participation and gave an idea of its scope.

Concerning the Louvre in Lens, the museum's architectural project contained extremely strong potential values. Its glass enclosure, for example, favored an "external" visit by a walk in the green space around the museum inviting an internal visit. The potential values created by this transparency provided unfamiliar museum residents to "tame" in the words of the architects while enjoying their walk. Beyond conventional communication to build awareness and image, all of these markers produce suggestive representations of what the offer can do to the beneficiaries. They are crucial elements in the strategic fight against intangibility.

In the case of Fes, the enclosure of the Bab Makina Palace is one of these markers. The potential values developed on this site, renowned for its acoustics, come essentially from the splendor of a heritage to be discovered.

The question about an offer can also come from the heterogeneity of resources that beneficiaries can combine with other stakeholders. Between understanding and expanding, recognizing these differences in resources can be an excellent way to deal with their possible tension. The availability of the offer according to the beneficiaries' resources is a key question on the MLP/SPT axes. Taking into account what age, cultural or income level and special area of interest create, as differences in resources to be combined is a factor in accepting the service offer.

For Lille3000, the conception of the days of the "fantastic" event is based on a spectacular appeal to all energies including, more particularly, those of children. Similarly, the shows by their roaming or the activities mixing both adults and children played on the transmission and complementarity of the resources to be combined (making clothes, carrying out a search, offering objects considered strange, etc.). The consideration of heterogeneity, the concern for bringing these differences in resources together, can be elements that sustain advancement. They allow the designers of the offer to set up mechanisms for the value co-creation in which the unexpected effects of the offer are manifested thanks to the creativity and innovative spirit of the beneficiaries.

From this point of view, the governance and regulation of the museum offer at the Louvre Lens makes heterogeneity one of the significant principles in extending the cultural theme to other beneficiary themes by promoting the concept of openness and accessibility to all. By the free and easy access to the permanent exhibition of the museum, the inhabitants of the territory in their cultural diversity can appropriate the museum for curiosity, meeting point, and quick and repeated glance to the works, which is far from the scheduled museum visit. To create exchange values, the heterogeneity of which is particularly promising as soon as it favors access. The Louvre uses an exhibition principle in Lens which is based on the exchanges that give rise to differences. Foreign audiences, even without cultural references, find descriptive sheets in two languages of the works with contextualization, the comparisons on the same theme of works from different civilizations. The children's routes taking advantage of these devices could understand the community of themes under the heterogeneity of plastic solutions depending on civilizations.

The festival of Fes, by retaining a positioning of the offer on sacred music typically targets a segment of the public whose expectations are highly cultural and conducive to heritage tourism and initiated that the forums and the medina make possible. The question about the heterogeneity of the offer does not suit this positioning strategy.

Chapter 5 on the CSV method emphasizes the importance of the question concerning the means of strengthening inseparability. It is a property of the service offering during the combination of resources at the supplier-beneficiary interface. It is lost as soon as the interface is completed. Extending inseparability is equivalent to maintaining contact with beneficiaries for as long as possible. Strategically maintaining inseparability consists of suggesting a maximum of values in use to beneficiaries likely to maintain contact.

It is clear that the "fantastic" festival, concentrated on the mobilization of interregional energies, relies on the associative fabric to maintain a creative alert among those who have experienced the festival and prepared for the next one, as well as the "madhouses" created in the neighborhoods of the city serving as relay points to maintain this contact. In this sense, creating inseparability is also ensuring, through digital or conventional means, links with the participants of the event. Databases such as social networks and platforms are becoming strategic places where designers can exchange ideas and observe modes of value creation brought about by the offer, which are essentially the result of innovation and the initiatives of these participants.

Inseparability is the place to question the value co-creation, a pivotal moment in the relationship between emerging and institutional or in the resolution, always to be reinvented, of the tensions between understanding and extension.

The Louvre's strategy also makes inseparability one of the key points of its strategy. How can the motivation of curiosity, which is by nature ephemeral, eventually come to dry up the flow of visitors? Renewal of temporary exhibitions, the creation of a platform for friends of the Louvre, the creation of a visitor database, regular administration of questionnaires on-site, the implementation of digital means of conversation from a digital site, and creation and initiation workshops are feasible applications so that the end of a visit is not the signal of a separation. The question of inseparability is present in the construction of the image of the Louvre Lens and its evoked set that links the museum to a whole series of occasions to visit. It is a source of inspiration for all governance and regulation of the territory.

The FWSMF intensely links the problem of inseparability to that of the extension of the residence time in the Fes, Meknes-Volubilis and Ifrane triangle. The reservation database of the festival provides ways to stay in touch with festival-goers. This database and the site presenting the festival program are all ways to revive the clientele segment targeted by the festival and to suggest a large number of trading and values in use in or around the city.

The last property in the service offer is that of perishability. The question concerns the loyalty of the beneficiaries when the service is rendered and has delivered its promised value in use. This loyalty building is strategic to conduct a long-term territorial development policy and manage the evolving relationships between the emerging and the institutional on the theme. The salience or keeping in mind of the beneficiaries of use is valuable once they have perished and from which they derive their appreciation of these values, as well as the exploitation of the positive externalities of these uses are at stake.

Lille3000, for example, uses benchmarks for each of the events it creates (popular parade, presentation in the heart of the city of the elements of the parade, rise of associations in the preparation of the event, etc.) capable of reactivating all the values delivered by the previous events. Likewise, Lille3000 seeks to collect positive externalities (animation ideas, costume making, use of objects found in landscaped excavations, etc.) where the beneficiaries co-create unforeseen uses to be reactivated during other events.

The fight against perishability directly nurtures the question of the co-creation of new values in use by the beneficiaries in identified externalities. They are new values in exchange or in use that the event can transfer or capture in a strategy for promoting initiatives or supporting unforeseen uses. In this specific case, an information system that tracks the uses and the assessments of these uses can extend the promised values making the beneficiary a co-creator. The Louvre in Lens, therefore, offers post-visit workshops where artistic co-creation reinforces and extends the values in use inspired by the visit.

In all three case studies, the information gathered by the Values Program mainly borrowed from TVF its key questions on the six steps of its survey methodology. The questions for each of these six steps served as references to build the focus group interview grids and individual interviews.

Thus, in step 1 the questions asked touch on the criteria for delimiting the territory allowing respondents to agree on the subject of their comments. It served as a common starting point for all interviews. The responses obtained for each territory ensure the consistency of a common territorial entity for all analyzes. Step 1 appears to be an essential prerequisite for the quality of the TVF application.

In Step 2 the questions asked are devoted to the choice of themes for territorial development. It was thus the subject of the interviews required by the objectives of the Values program. The theme common to all the talks was that of cultural development. The open questions replaced the cultural theme in the challenges of territorial development. The perceived importance of the theme by the respondents, the interpretation of the context in terms of opportunities for the chosen theme, the capacity of the territory to seize these opportunities and to avoid threats, the statement of the territorial choices of cultural policy have all served to focus analysis and interpretation on the theme of the place and role of cultural policy in the development of each of the three territories.

Step 3 was a key step in the qualitative interviews. The questions asked invited respondents to identify the stakeholders in the theme of culture by first speaking spontaneously and then attempting to classify these stakeholders according to the characteristics described in chapter 4. The discussion then turned to the concepts of Power, Urgency and Legitimacy and on the seven dynamics of territorial development presented in this same chapter. Each speaker was able, using the TVF methodology and diagrams, to provide their conception of the relational functions maintained by the stakeholders identified above. The issue of stakeholder relations in governance was central. It brought together the concrete elements capable of feeding into the summaries proposed in Figures 4.4 and 3.3 on the respective situations of the three territories according to their capacity to lead territorial development.

In step 4: Once familiar with the general approach of TVF, the questions asked to the respondents, in this step 4, sought to know their opinion on the current governance and regulation of the cultural theme in their territory. This step is the most political of the investigation. It often elicited lengthy comments. The use of the MicMac and Mactor methods is essential here. Participants are invited to choose among the variables provided by the TVF those deemed essential for the theme and to identify their interactions. Following the processing of their responses, a summary was submitted to their comments for validation. It resulted in a modelisable system of interactions between the selected variables. Based on this system used to describe the initial situation in which each territory is led to conduct its cultural policy, a prospective approach is proposed to the respondents. They are invited to propose and validate several possible cultural development scenarios for their territory. According to the orientations and objectives of each scenario, an analysis of the places and roles of the stakeholders involved can be carried out using the MacTor method. A mapping of these places and roles of stakeholders is carried out. It can then be discussed with the territorial actors in order to establish the most suitable strategy.

In Step 5: The step seeks to know how the chosen strategic orientations are materialized by the construction of territorial offers. The questions asked are inspired by the tools of the CSV and the stakeholders. As pointed out above this step could not be developed in this book. This step 5 is clearly devoted to the regulation which engages certain stakeholders in the process of combining resources and co-production to achieve territorial offers. This offer proposition must materialize the theme's development objectives. The identification of the stakeholders necessary for the realization of each offer is carried out. Their modes of combining resources and co-production are analyzed. Their optimization or even their extensions to other stakeholders are discussed. The examination of territorial offers with a constant concern for improvement and innovation is based on the references of the twelve sensitive points of the CSV. Likewise, the questions of the beneficiaries' resources to be combined, the role of stakeholders as "prior integrators » in the construction of the offer and the potential values, values in exchange and values in use in the promise of the offer are debated. Working groups can thus find in the CSV and the stakeholder analysis the methodological framework, developed in this book, to enrich the propositions for action and ensure the adaptation of the offer by the IHIP model. From then on, an action plan can be built and shared.

In step 6: This step is oriented towards feedback and an ex post evaluation of the overall approach. It is carried out by the analyst, in relation to the stakeholders around issues related to the preparation and implementation of the process. It concludes with an analytical report, a capitalization of experience and propositions.

Bibliography

Cox, K. R. 1997. Spaces and Globalization, Reasserting the Power of the Local, 292. New York, Guilford Publications Inc.

Cox, K. R. 2011. "Institutions of Local and Regional Development." in *A Handbook of Local and Regional Development*, edited by A Pike, A Rodrigues-Pose and J Tomaney, Chapter 23. Routledge.

Howard, J. A. 1969. "Marketing Management: Analysis and Planning.", In *Homewood, the theory of buyer Behavior*, edited by R Irwin. New-York: Wiley.

Godet, M. and Durance, P. 2011. *La prospective stratégique pour les entreprises et les territoires* 2e édition. Paris. Dunod.

Conclusion

The Territorial Value Framework (TVF) provides analysts and policymakers with a general approach and the sources of which can be identified in all of the references delivered in the book. The essential objective of the TVF is to offer, beyond all these contributions, a synthetic vision of territorial development problems in order to identify the nature of multiple obstacles to development and the solutions to overcome them.

This overall vision is only possible by researching the essentials of the interactions that drive the governance and regulation of the territory. The TVF shows that, in the territory, these two essential dimensions of the conduct of development are not fixed. Governance in the MLP/SPT approach can be observed in a territory in the multiple forms that characterize the legal, the normative, but also the emerging. When governance is concerned with "making actors", the TVF affirms as essential for the development dynamic to set up information systems capable of capturing the emerging and adopting governance systems where it can have a role.

Likewise, regulation cannot be understood only as the operational arm of development objectives. The TVF defines regulation as inseparable from governance in understanding the dynamics of development. This inseparability can be read in all the interpretive figures of the TVF using vectorization and crossing. The explanation comes from the fact that the TVF regards regulation as a moment of combining resources that involves both providers and beneficiaries on all the propositions for territorial offers. In the TVF, the inseparability between governance and regulation comes from the role that offer propositions play in managing the reduction of tensions between the multiple forms of legal, normative and emerging.

In this sense, governance management is a management of the modes of value creation and their attractiveness as the engine of the general dynamics of development of a territory. Regulation is thus an active approach to combining and transforming resources, and the effects of which come directly from governance and not from operational performance alone.

The TVF seeks to assess the development dynamics of a territory using an indicator, the external validity of which is assumed to be strong. This indicator aims to contribute to the overall vision of territorial development issues by introducing a reference to energy and to the motivation of exchanges into the interpretative system. The concept of tension proposed by the TVF represents this reference. It should be understood by analysts and policymakers as an invitation to listen to creativity whatever its content is. This tension is thus described by the TVF as an expression, useful for any development dynamic, of the struggle for legitimacy. The proposed reading grid points out the tension between understanding the circumstances and the details of the application of a project and the extension where the general and responsible application of this project is sought.

The analysts can synthesize a given situation of the tensions between emerging and institutional in a territory by using Tables 3.1, 3.2 and 3.3 that present the typology of the nine profiles of territorial development proposed by the TVF. These tables observe, in this tension, the engine of the debate that should build the development of the territory. This debate is about responsibility and value propositions. Within the limits of presentation of the case studies in this work, the TVF methods were applied systematically from the first five steps proposed by the method. And this conclusion can be considered the sixth and the last step.

Only one development theme was selected. It is clear that the method asks the analyst to make an exhaustive inventory of the development themes present in the territorial plan, which is the focus of the analysis. These themes can be the subject of a separate analysis; however, certain themes can appear as the expression of the positioning of the territory. They are then interpreted as promising themes, and the joint effects of which on other themes should be measured. The three examples in Chapter 7 show that certain themes can play a triggering role that should be supported to obtain all the expected effects. It is the task for the analyst to reveal the contextual opportunities and find their best use in precise territorial positioning.

The three cases show that the opportunities to be exploited for the territories fundamentally relate to geographic opportunities and mobility exploitation. Other contexts can direct other themes to play this positioning role. In this case, the thinking of the evoked set or the notion of destination recommended by the TVF can remain fruitful for themes that would relate to, for example, the economy, society or environment. The territory's ability to define opportunities to take advantage of is the responsibility of governance and its information systems. Figure 4.4 shows how the dynamics of the territory is in search of a strategy that can be initiated by a few stakeholders. To advance in the analysis, it is necessary to observe how the types and the number of involved stakeholders evolve. It is also important to know the dynamics, among the seven proposed ones, that these stakeholders animate. Under this consideration, the three cases show the importance given by the TVF to this notion of development dynamics and their relational functions that support them. In all three cases, in different forms, these relational functions have evolved not only in number but in negotiation content.

Beyond the simple census, only does the functional approach decide on the strengths and weaknesses of the involved stakeholders to take advantage of the opportunities identified. The question of the available resources of stakeholders becomes crucial to deal with the capacity to exploit these opportunities. The functional analysis proposed by the TVF must explore the use made of governance and regulation to reach propositions for reducing tensions. This analysis is put into practice according to the seven dynamics proposed in Figure 4.3 and the requirements of the eight types of stakeholders. At this stage, the diagnosis of the territory's dynamics can be performed based on the noticeable absence, among the eight stakeholders or the seven dynamics, that can be mobilized on each development theme. The relational functions established by the diagnosis lead to understanding the modes of resolution of the tensions that the theme has reached.

From this point of view, the functional analysis of each theme of territorial development should help to characterize this theme. It can be in terms of general development dynamics by following Figure 4.4. The TVF characterizes, for each of the themes carried by the territory, its dynamic capacity with respect to territorial development. This positioning of each theme in one of the four quartiles allows, in a systemic vision, measuring the coherence of a global dynamic. The functional analysis of the TVF, therefore, must pay particular attention to the content of the relational functions of the stakeholders. Also, it should establish whether at the qualitative level (negotiated decisions of offer proposition, methods of creating value, etc.) as well as at the quantitative level (presence of stakeholders and the relational functions that connect them, etc.) the contributing characteristics of development are present in a territory. The analysis of the content of relational functions should help analysts to decide on their state of divergence and their weak legitimacy where tensions can accumulate as a power relationship relatively exacerbated by the urgency. This state of divergence and struggle for legitimacy marks the three quartiles of crisis highlighted in Figure 4.4.

At the heart of the evaluation system, the question of the nature and methods of value creation must help to finalize the diagnosis of the development dynamic and the recommendations for future territorial policies. The Cube Service Value (CSV) establishes whether the offer propositions reconcile a strategic (governance) and operational (regulation) perspective. Through potential values and values in exchange, governance reinforces the inseparability of strategic and operational. The use of these values reinvents new relational functions with stakeholders that have been dormant or not taken into account so far.

The analysts are asked by the TVF to observe in depth how governance and regulation develop strategic and operational thinking. It is by considering the inseparability and the perishability of territorial offer propositions that the conditions for adaptation and territorial development are created to demonstrate strong legitimacy.

Index

www.ingramcontent.com/pod-product-compliance
Lightning Source LLC
Chambersburg PA
CBHW050516280326
41932CB00014B/2337